GUIDE FOR THE NEW ZEALAND TRAVELLER IN BRITAIN

By John McLean

This book is sold subject to the condition that it shall not, by way of trade or otherwise, be loaned, re-sold, hired out or otherwise circulated without the publisher's prior written consent, in any form of binding or cover other than that in which it is published and without a similar condition, including this condition, being imposed on the subsequent purchaser.

While every effort has been made to ensure that the information contained herein is accurate neither the publisher nor the author will accept any responsibility resulting from inaccurate information; in other words, if you drive twenty miles over rough roads only to find that the castle has just been blown up by the neighbouring chief during a clan feud, don't sue the author.

Copyright © John McLean, 2002

Cover: The Household Cavalry passing under the arches at Hyde Park Corner, London.

Published by Winter Productions,
37b New Cavendish Street, London W1G 8JR &
27 Euston Road, Wadestown, Wellington, New Zealand.

ISBN 1 872970 09 5

Printed through Colorcraft Ltd., Hong Kong
for Winter Productions,
37b New Cavendish Street, London W1G 8JR

To my sister,

Jane McLean

INTRODUCTION

A New Zealander travelling to Britain is not just going to another country but to the land from which New Zealand was discovered and settled. Most New Zealanders can trace their ancestry back to their British forbears while our institutions, system of government, rights and freedoms, common law, language and even games all derive from Great Britain. No nation exists in isolation and there is no country which has had a greater impact on the founding, development and character of New Zealand than the United Kingdom. Indeed, it is not possible to understand New Zealand's history, literature or system of government without being aware of their British roots.

There are in all parts of the British Isles places and things that were and are part of the New Zealand story but which travellers are likely to miss through lack of information. The purpose of this book is to bring to the attention of the traveller monuments where famous New Zealanders are commemorated, war cemeteries where Anzacs are buried, ports from which both discoverers and colonists set out in tiny sailing ships for the other side of the world, works of art by New Zealanders and other places of interest like the school in London that Katherine Mansfield attended and the pub in Cardiff where ex-All Black Keith Murdoch punched the doorman. By highlighting links with one's own country and, in many cases, with one's home town (See: Index of New Zealand towns), this guide will make a

New Zealander's trip to Britain more meaningful and memorable.

Just as New Zealand has characteristics not to be found in Britain – geysers, glaciers and pavlovas – so too does Britain have a lot of treasures not to be found in New Zealand – castles, pageantry, world class museums and art galleries and, of course, lots of cosy country pubs with their log fires and real ale.

It is also the home of our beautiful English language and the countryside is dotted with the shrines of literature – places like Shakespeare's birthplace, Wordsworth's cottage in the Lake District and the little churchyard at Stoke Poges where Gray wrote his famous elegy.

All the history of Britain before our forbears sailed to New Zealand is our history too; things like the Reformation, the English Civil War and the Industrial Revolution left their marks and affected the type of society that was later set up in New Zealand.

I have stuck to the traditional county boundaries with which New Zealanders are more likely to be familiar. Enjoy your travelling and sightseeing and remember that what you get out of your visit to Britain depends largely on what you bring with you in your heart and mind. Although Britain is as far away from New Zealand as it is possible to go, there is probably no other place in the world where a New Zealander will feel more at home.

OTHER BOOKS WRITTEN BY JOHN McLEAN

Fiction:

Island of the Gods (578 pages). Set on the island of Bali this classic love story describes the adventures of Adrian, a Western surfer, and Dayu, a Balinese village girl. Price: £6 or NZ$20. - "It's a good read. He's a natural storyteller" – Hong Kong Standard.

Deep Inside (198 pages). Eighteen short stories about many aspects of surfing. Price: £5 or NZ$16.

Tartan Dragon (554 pages) Set in colonial Hong Kong, a saga of three generations of a Scottish contracting dynasty who built Hong Kong. Price: £7 or NZ$20

Traffic Jam (173 pages) A hilarious desription of a week-end when London gets jammed with a million vehicles. Gridlock, horror and comedy. Price: £4 or NZ$12.

Non-fiction:

English Phonics (65 pages) Teaching English to children by the traditional means of phonetics (sounds). Price: £8 or NZ$ 22.

Tyranny of the Law (281 pages). A frightening expose of how the law is intruding into people's lives in a step-by-step process. Written for the layman. Price: £8 or NZ$22. – "In to-day's politically correct climate McLean's book is radical and refreshing". – Freedom To-day magazine, London.

Cheques payable to "Winter Productions", 37b New Cavendish Street, London W1G 8JR or 27 Euston Road, Wadestown, Wellington, New Zealand. All prices include postage.

Since Britain is a much older country than New Zealand it has many more styles of architecture that represent different periods. The following glossary should be of use to those who visit some of these beautiful buildings.

Norman (called "Romanesque" in Europe) 1066-1154: Great semi-circular arches supported on large, round pillars. Thick walls with small windows and doors. Simple vaulting and much carving of detail. Durham Cathedral is the finest example. Also Saint Alban's Cathedral.

Early English: The first period of Gothic (13th century). Thinner walls, pointed arches and buttresses. An important feature is the pointed lancet windows either singly or in groups. Early English is Gothic in its purest and simplest form, e.g. Salisbury Cathedral, the Nave of Lincoln Cathedral and the Chapter House at Westminster Abbey.

Decorated or High Gothic (c.1290-1350): The advance in engineering skills brought about the soaring pointed arch. Windows became sub-divided with complex geometrical figures in their upper reaches.

Perpendicular or Late Gothic (15th century): With the further development of engineering knowledge the walls could now be thin and the windows wide and tall. This made for greater space and more light, e.g. King's College Chapel, Cambridge, the cloisters of Gloucester

Cathedral, the Naves of Canterbury and Winchester Cathedrals and Henry VI's Chapel in Westminster Abbey.

Tudor: The latest form of the Perpendicular, 1485-1603. Noted for its broad arches which replaced the Gothic pointed arches. Often rich in heraldic imagery – things like roses and pomegranates.

Palladian: Named after the work of Andrea Palladio (1518-1580). Imitation of ancient Roman architecture without regard to classical principles. Introduced to Britain in the seventeenth century.

Baroque: A florid style of late Renaissance architecture of the seventeenth and eighteenth centuries that was inspired by the buildings of ancient Greece and Rome, e.g. Saint Paul's Cathedral in London.

Jacobean (of the reign of James I – 1603-1625): A style incorporating very late Gothic with Palladian. Very ornamental and often featuring curved gables. One of the best examples of Jacobean architecture is Hatfield House, Hertfordshire, which was built between 1607 and 1612.

Queen Anne: (1702-14) A liberal use of red brick facings on houses and buildings. Tall sash windows and roofs hidden behind parapets. Noted for its plain style and dignified restraint.

Georgian (covering the reigns of the first four King Georges, 1714–1830) Various styles of Palladian with unadorned window and door frames. Robert Adam was the foremost architect in this period.

Regency: Named after the Prince Regent, who later became King George IV, this represents the flowering at the end of the Georgian period. George IV was a great patron of architecture and some of London's finest buildings were crafted during this time (1810-30) The period was noted for the influence of neo-Classical motifs and the results were both opulent and beautiful. The main architect of the period was John Nash.

PARTS OF A CHURCH

Nave: The main body of a church or cathedral

Transept: When a cathedral is built in the shape of a cross, the Transepts are the two arms of the cross on either side of the Nave, running north and south; they are always north and south since every cathedral in Britain (except Coventry) faces east towards Bethlehem.

Chancel: The space in a church reserved for the officiating clergy and the choir. It is usually between the altar and the nave and is often separated from the rest of the church by a screen or railing.

Reredos: The ornamental facing on the wall behind the altar.

Choir: The part of a church (usually in the chancel) that is allotted to the singers.

Apse: A large semi-circular or polygonal recess that usually has arches and a domed roof and is at the end of the nave or choir.

Cloisters: A covered walkway (usually arched) along the sides of a quadrangle of a monastery, abbey or other building devoted to religious seclusion.

TITLES

Since there are many references to titled people in this volume I have decided to list below the various titles in descending order of importance.

Prince and Princess: Children of the monarch and of the heir to the throne are princes and princesses.

Duke and Duchess: A duke is the highest title for any non-member of the Royal Family. However, some members of the Royal Family also bear this title and are known as "royal dukes", e.g. Prince Philip, the husband of the Queen, is the Duke of Edinburgh while the Queen's second son, Prince Andrew, is Duke of York. Two of her royal cousins are the Duke of Kent and the Duke of Gloucester; these titles will be familiar to Shakespearean scholars as being characters from his historical plays. Altogether there are about forty dukes in Britain.

Marquess and Marchioness: Note that the word "Marquess" is spelt differently from its counterpart in France where it is "Marquis". An heir to a dukedom can have the title of Marquess until his father dies and he becomes the new duke. Others are a Marquess in their own right.

Earl and Countess: One would think that the husband of a Countess should be a Count – as in Europe – but, like so many other things in Britain, aristocratic titles have their fair share of idiosyncracies. An earl often takes his title from a place; thus the former Governor of

New Zealand, after whom Wellington's Glasgow Wharf is named, was David Boyle, 7th Earl of Glasgow.

Viscount and Viscountess: In France a viscount is literally a "vice count" (deputy count). However, in Britain, where the title of count does not exist, a viscountcy is a highly regarded title.

Baron and Baroness: This also has its equivalent in France. It is the lowest of the hereditary titles of the peerage.

Lord and Lady: The word "Lord" indicates that either its holder is a member of the House of Lords or that he bears it only as a courtesy title, being the son of an earl, marquess or duke. Everyone with the title of Baron or higher is also a lord and is often referred to as Lord X rather than Viscount X.

Sir: This is the title for a knight and his wife is a Lady, e.g. Sir Peter and Lady Blake. There are several orders of knighthood, the Garter being the highest order in England and the Thistle being the highest order in Scotland. When Robert Menzies, Prime Minister of Australia from 1949 to 1966, was knighted he was given the Thistle rather than the Garter because he was of Scottish descent.

There are two types of knighthood: hereditary and non-hereditary. A hereditary knight is called a Baronet and puts the abbreviated letters "Bt." after his name. When the Queen wishes to confer the equivalent of a knighthood on a woman, she makes her a Dame, e.g. Dame Malvina Major.

CHAPTERS

London

	Page
The West End	17
Inns Of Court and the City	29
The East End	51
South London	56
Whitehall and Westminster	61
Parks and Palaces	75
West London	84
North London	92
Greenwich and the Thames	96

Countryside – England

Kent	101
Sussex	103
Surrey	108
Berkshire	117
Hampshire	128
Dorset	135
Wiltshire	136
Devon	139
Cornwall	147
Somerset	155
Gloucestershire	156
Hertfordshire	159
Cambridgeshire	160
Huntingdonshire	173
Northamptonshire	174

Leicestershire	174
Oxfordshire	175
Warwickshire	186
Worcestershire	195
Shropshire	199
Herefordshire	200
Staffordshire	201
Derbyshire	207
Nottinghamshire	210
Lincolnshire	211
Cheshire	216
Liverpool	216
Lancashire	219
Manchester	222
Yorkshire	224
Durham	235
Northumberland	242

Scotland

Dumfries	248
Ayrshire	251
Renfrewshire	256
Glasgow	256
Dunbartonshire	258
Edinburgh	259
East Lothian	266
Fife	267
Grampians	268
Angus	268
Aberdeenshire	270

Argyll   270
Ross   276
Sutherland   278
Shetland Islands   279

Wales

Glamorgan   280
Carmarthen   282
Pembroke   283

Northern Ireland

Belfast   284
Antrim   285
Londonderry   286

Channel Islands   288

While every endeavour has been made to ensure that the information contained herein is up to date it would be appreciated if any changes could be brought to our attention.

The bronze bust of Lord Freyberg, V.C. which graces the front lobby of New Zealand House, London. Crafted by the eminent sculptor, Oscar Nemon, it was presented by the New Zealand community in London at a ceremony at the Guildhall on 25th July, 1962

THE WEST END

"A door had opened and England was before us – old, gracious and lovely."

- Alan Mulgan, author of *Home – A New Zealander's Adventure*

Since the great glass structure of New Zealand House is right in the heart of London there is no better place to begin a tour of the West End.

The site in the Haymarket on which New Zealand House stands was formerly occupied by both a theatre and the Carlton Hotel which latter was bombed in the Second World War. The present sixteen storey building, designed by Robert Matthew, was completed in 1963 when it was opened by the Queen. It is now listed as an historic building since it is regarded as a prime example of Sixties glass and concrete architecture! There are magnificent views of London from its roof terrace.

The lobby is dominated by a 51 foot high Maori carving that was crafted out of a single totara tree, which was felled in New Zealand and transported in three pieces. Upon arrival in Britain each piece was cut in half and the finished product is held together by a steel cable that runs through its whole length from its base to the ceiling of the third floor.

It was carved by the singer, Inia Te Wiata, who started work on it in the basement of New Zealand House in 1964. However, he could work on it only between singing engagements and he died before finishing the last part, which was the second of the two canoe prows. His two sons completed the task.

In the rear of the lobby is a bronze bust of Lord Freyberg V.C., the former Governor-General. Sculpted by Oscar Nemon, it was presented by the New Zealand community in London. Freyberg, an old boy of Wellington College, was widely regarded as the bravest soldier in the British Empire although some said that he shared the honour with another Victoria Cross winner, the dashing, one-eyed British general, Sir Carton de Wiart.

Inside the High Commission building is the office of New Zealand News, a free newspaper which is published in Britain every Wednesday and contains news items from New Zealand during the previous week. In the ornate Royal Opera Arcade behind the High Commission is the Kiwifruits shop which sells books, giftware and other products from New Zealand.

Across the road from the entrance of New Zealand House and a few yards along Pall Mall is Trafalgar Square. Three of the monuments in this great open space are dedicated to men whose names are remembered in New Zealand towns. The square is dominated by Nelson standing atop his 185 foot high Column which, like the city of Nelson at the top of the South Island, is a tribute to Britain's greatest sailor who fell in his moment of glory at Trafalgar, the great sea victory that ensured the survival and stability of the British Empire for decades to come.

In the south-west corner (near Canada House) is a statue of General Sir Charles Napier (1782-1853) after whom Napier in the Hawkes Bay was named. He fought in the Peninsula War against the French during which he was wounded six times and had two horses killed from under him! He finished up as commander-in-chief of the Indian Army. In India he defeated a much larger Indian force at Meeanee (also a town in the Hawkes Bay) and this gave him control of the province of Sind which he ruled humanely, abolishing slavery and suttee (widow burning) and creating the port of Karachi. This grandson of a duke was commissioned in the army at the age of eleven! He was a bluff soldier who was popular with his men. The statue here in Trafalgar Square was paid for by public subscription, most of the contributions coming from private soldiers.

The word "Napier" is a Scottish expression meaning "no equal". In the thirteenth century the King of the Scots, Alexander III, told a brave soldier called Lennox that he had "nae peer" as a warrior ("no equal"). The soldier was given land in Fife and East Lothian and was told to go there and take his new name with him. Over the following centuries the family produced a succession of fine soldiers who proudly bore the new name while the people of Napier in the Hawkes Bay believe that their garden city has "nae peer".

At the other end of the Square (south-east corner) is a magnificent statue of General Sir Henry Havelock who led the small force that relieved the British Residency at Lucknow during the Indian Mutiny in 1857. However, he himself became trapped in the

Statue of General Napier, Trafalgar Square, London
Photograph: John Bate-Williams
In Trafalgar Square are statues of three men after whom New Zealand towns are named – Napier, Nelson and Havelock.

Residency with his troops and so a second relieving army had to be sent. Havelock, a teetotaller, died shortly after his moment of triumph. Besides his statue here in the heart of London his name is remembered in the towns of Havelock North in the Hawkes Bay and Havelock in the Marlborough Sounds.

On the wall of Trafalgar Square, below the road in front of the National Gallery, are three bronze busts of famous sailors. The one in the middle is of Admiral of the Fleet Earl Jellicoe (1859-1935). In the First World War he commanded the British fleet at the Battle of Jutland, the most crucial naval battle of the war. After the War he was Governor-General of New Zealand between 1920 and 1924.

Not surprisingly for a naval officer who reached the supreme office of First Sea Lord, Jellicoe was a keen yachtsman and, during his time in New Zealand, he took part in the first Sanders Cup series. He used to sail on Auckland Harbour in a 14 foot yacht that was named *Iron Duke* – after the name of the Dreadnought that was his flagship in the Battle of Jutland! The Jellicoe Channel, between Little Barrier Island and Cape Rodney, is named after him.

At the side of the National Gallery in Saint Martin's Place is the entrance to the National Portrait Gallery. On the Top Floor in Room 13 ("Science and Industry") is a portrait of Sir Joseph Banks, the botanist who sailed with Captain Cook on the *Endeavour* and after whom Banks Peninsula is named.

In Room 14 ("Britain Becomes a World Power") is a painting of Captain Cook by John Webber, who was a Swiss draughtsman on Cook's third and last voyage to the Pacific. There is also a portrait of King George III in whose name Captain Cook claimed New Zealand for the British Crown. Another painting of interest in this Room is that of Warren Hastings (1732-1818), the Governor-General of India after whom the Hawkes Bay city of Hastings is named. Nearby is a portrait of Robert Clive of India after whom the Hawkes Bay town of Clive is named. The First Floor features subjects of the Victorian era and the early twentieth century. In the Statesman's Gallery is a bust of the Duke of Wellington, after whom New Zealand's capital city was named.

The next bust is of Lord John Russell, Prime Minister of Great Britain from 1846 to 1852, in whose honour was named New Zealand's first capital, the historic town of Russell in North Auckland.

The next bust is of Richard Cobden, the leader of the Anti-Corn Law League, whose name is remembered in the town of Cobden, across the Grey River from Greymouth on the West Coast.

At the end of the Statesman's Gallery is the famous painting by Sir James Guthrie of the British and imperial leaders of the First World War. The Prime Minister of New Zealand, William Massey, is in the foreground, sitting at the table in a black suit with his back partly to the viewer. He is recognised by his thick white moustache and balding head. The attendance of the empire prime ministers at the Versailles Peace Conference in 1919 was significant in that it was the first time that New Zealand and the other dominions had been represented at an international conference in their own right.

In the other group portrait of the First World War generals by Sir John Sargent the first man on the left is General Sir William Birdwood (1885-1951), who was commander of the Anzacs at Gallipoli.

On the other side of the room (above the head of the statue of a reclining Lawrence of Arabia) is a portrait of Admiral Jellicoe who, as we have seen, was Governor-General of New Zealand. Above Lawrence's feet is a painting of Field-Marshal Allenby under whose command the Australian and New Zealand forces fought in Palestine in the First World War.

The next room, Room 27, has several portraits that are of interest to New Zealanders. On the left as you enter is a picture of Lord Newall, Marshal of the Royal Air Force, who was Governor-General of New Zealand from 1941 to 1946.

Nearby is a painting of the familiar figure of Field-Marshal Montgomery who commanded the Eighth Army in the North African desert including, of course, the New Zealand Division. Monty is standing in front of a map of Europe with his finger pointing appropriately to Normandy. On his head is the trademark beret with the two cap badges that he always wore; one badge was the emblem of the Royal Tank Regiment and the other the hat badge of a general. The victor of Alamein visited New Zealand after the War and was received with acclamation wherever he went.

Next to the victor of Alamein is a portrait of Sir Archibold McIndoe (1900-1960), the Dunedin born surgeon who, from his hospital at East Grinstead in Sussex, remade the faces of hundreds of R.A.F. airmen who had been severely burned in the air battles of the Second World War. McIndoe also did plastic surgery on air raid victims from London and the south-east. (See: East Grinstead)

Above the McIndoe portrait is that of one of his patients, Richard Hillary, an R.A.F. pilot who was shot down in the Battle of Britain and had to have extensive plastic surgery to his face. He returned to active service but was later killed in an air crash in 1943.

A few feet further along is a painting of Lord Rutherford (1871-1937), the Spring Grove (Nelson) born genius whose experiments led to the splitting of the atom in 1932. Next to him is one of the loveliest paintings in the Gallery – a conversation piece of the Royal family sitting around a table having afternoon tea – "Us four" as King George VI used to call them.

A left turn outside the entrance of the National Portrait Gallery will take you into Charing Cross Road. Cross at the first pedestrian crossing and you will be outside the Charing Cross Library. During the Second World War this building was the New Zealand Forces Club and was open to all members of the Allied Forces. There is a plaque inside the door which records the gratitude of the government and people of New Zealand to the hundreds of workers who gave their services here during those fateful years.

Behind the buildings on the other side of Charing Cross Road is the pedestrianised Leicester Square. On the eastern side of the square (nearest

Charing Cross Road) is the Odeon Cinema where the New Zealand made film, Lord of the Rings, had its world premiere in December, 2001.

Continuing up Charing Cross Road, past all the famous bookshops, you reach its junction with Oxford Street. One block south-west of this busy corner is Soho Square, a small area of greenery that is dominated by the Tudor style house in the middle of its lawns. The word "Soho" derives from a hunting cry – "So Ho"; it is believed that hares and foxes were once hunted here.

In the south-west corner of the square at Number 32 is Twentieth Century House, the offices of Twentieth Century Fox Film Studios. At right angles to its entrance is a not very distinctive engraving in the concrete wall which states that on this site stood the home of Sir Joseph Banks (1743-1820), the botanist who accompanied Captain Cook to New Zealand on the *Endeavour* and after whom Banks Peninsula in Canterbury is named. At the time that he charted the New Zealand coast Cook thought that this peninsula was an island and he named it Banks Island. When it was later found to be a peninsula, it became Banks Peninsula.

Rich, lively and a keen amateur scientist, Banks was only twenty-four when he joined the *Endeavour*. At the time his wealthy friends urged him to make a Grand Tour of Europe which was the fashionable thing to do at the time. "Every blockhead does that", replied Banks. "My grand tour will be around the globe." And so it was.

When the *Endeavour* was anchored in Queen Charlotte Sound at the top of the South Island Banks took specimens of all the native plants and took them back to England in packing cases. Despite the difference in their backgrounds, he and Captain Cook became lifelong friends.

Sir Joseph Banks moved to this house in Soho Square in 1777 and established an excellent library on natural history. In 1778 he was elected to the prestigious position of President of the Royal Society. During the protests against the Corn Laws his house was attacked by rioters and he died shortly afterwards of gout that was caused by excessive eating and drinking. Although his house no longer exists one can get some idea of the view over the square that he enjoyed – save for that twentieth century invention, the internal combustion engine.

Proceeding along Oxford Street in a westerly direction one comes to Oxford Circus. After crossing Regent Street the first street running south from Oxford Street is Harewood Place which leads into elegant Hanover Square. Leading off the square to the south is Saint George Street which is dominated by the church of Saint George's, a fashionable venue for society weddings. This beautiful church is worth a visit for its own sake but for New Zealanders there is an added interest for it was here that George Augustus Selwyn, the first Bishop of New Zealand (from 1842 to 1868) was ordained a priest in 1834. This was also the church where Lord Onslow, who became Governor of New Zealand in 1890, was married in 1875.

On the other (northern) side of Oxford Street is Cavendish Square. Leading north from this leafy oasis is Harley Street where some of Britain's leading doctors have their surgeries. Outside the Georgian buildings of Numbers 43-49 Harley Street one can see a green and white flag billowing in the breeze. This is Queen's College, founded as a girls' school more than 150 years ago. Based on a Christian socialist ethos it has never required its pupils to wear uniforms. To-day it is an independent school for girls aged between eleven and eighteen. This was the school where Katherine Mansfield received her secondary education. She arrived in 1903 at the age of fourteen with her two sisters, Vera and Charlotte. Her London based cousins, the Paynes, were already pupils there.

During her three years at the school she lived next door at No. 41 with about forty other boarders, sharing a room with her sisters which looked over the rooftops of London. The relaxed discipline of this modern (by the standards of the times) school right in the heart of cosmopolitan London and only a few minutes from the shops of Oxford Street and the flesh spots of Soho must have seemed like a world away from the small town colonial life of Wellington where she was born into a wealthy family that was ruled with a rod of iron by a stern Victorian father. This was her first introduction to London, a city she grew to love.

At Queen's College she studied German, French, English, singing and the cello. She also joined the school debating society. More importantly, she wrote short stories for the school magazine, using her middle name, "Mansfield", for the first time as her *nom de plume*. Her real surname was Beauchamp. This was the beginning of her writing career. Copies of these short stories are held in the school library and serious K.M. scholars who wish to see them may contact the librarian on Tel. 7291-7000 or the Senior Tutor. The part of the library devoted to the Internet is called the Katherine Mansfield Room.

In the old common room is the fireplace (no longer used because of post-war regulations against chimney smoke) of which she wrote "the leaping fires in winter".

This talented yet turbulent character was not popular with the other girls who regarded her as "moody".

After leaving Queen's College she returned to New Zealand for two years but in 1908 she was back in London where she became part of the "Bloomsbury set", a group of literary snobs who flattered and cheated each other while looking down their noses on the rest of mankind.

Continuing west along Oxford Street turn right into Portman Street which is the second to last turn before Marble Arch Underground Station. This leads into Gloucester Place and there is a blue plaque outside No. 48 which is of particular interest to people from Canterbury. This is the house where John Robert Godley (1814-61), widely regarded as the architect of the Canterbury settlement, lived and died. The northern headland of Lyttelton Harbour is named Godley Head in his honour and, of course, there is that fine statue of him in the heart of Christchurch, facing the Cathedral. Like Wakefield he wanted to create an orderly and well-balanced society representing all classes. The result of this worthy dream was the success of the Canterbury settlement.

INNS OF COURT AND THE CITY

"When a man is tired of London, he is tired of life for there is in London all that life can afford".

- Doctor Johnson

Proceeding east from Trafalgar Square along the Strand you will see a small street, Adam Street, running down to the river. Outside Nos. 1-5 at the bottom of the street is a plaque which states, "From offices on this site the New Zealand Company on 5th May, 1839, despatched the survey ship *Tory* to begin the colonisation of New Zealand on the Wakefield Plan." The plaque was placed here by the New Zealand Historic Places Trust.

The next turn on the right is Savoy Court which leads to the world famous Savoy Hotel where New Zealand Prime Ministers have traditionally stayed on their visits to London for Coronations and Commonwealth Prime Ministers' conferences. Kiri Te Kanawa used to stay here when she was performing at Covent Garden rather than go back to her home in Surrey at the end of each evening.

The Savoy is the closest hotel to the Royal Opera House, Covent Garden, which is situated in Bow Street, north of the Strand. The word "Covent" is a variation of "Convent"; until the seventeenth century this area was the garden of Westminster Abbey but in 1680 King Charles II, the Merry Monarch who fell in love with the actress, Nell Gwynne, granted a licence for a playhouse and performances have been held on the site ever since although the present Royal Opera House dates only from 1857.

Another New Zealander who sang at Covent Garden is Dame Malvina Major who played Rosalinda in *Die Fledermaus* in 1991. For her debut she wore a black velvet dress trimmed with gold; it was hand-made by the Hamilton Operatic Society and presented to her for the occasion. After the performance both Kiri Te Kanawa and Dame Joan Sutherland went backstage to congratulate her. A meeting of the three Dames!

Continuing along the Strand one sees two churches standing on their own islands. The second of these, opposite the impressive edifice of Australia House, is Saint Clement Danes.

The present church, designed by Sir Christopher Wren in 1682, was gutted by German bombers on 10th May, 1941, and only the outer walls and steeple were left standing. After the War it was restored and it reopened on 19th October, 1958, as the official church of the Royal Air Force.

According to tradition there has been a church on this site since the ninth century. It is, in fact, the church that was mentioned in the nursery rhyme

Saint Clement Danes, The Strand, London
Photograph: Kenneth Allen
This familiar and much loved London landmark contains several memorials to New Zealand airmen.

"Oranges and Lemons, the Bells of Saint Clement's" and indeed the bells ring out the tune every day at 9 a.m., noon, 3 p.m. and 6 p.m. The song is believed to refer to a medieval custom of distributing these citrus fruits to the people as a cure for scurvy.

Upon entering this beautiful and spacious church you will see, set into the floor, a rosette of the badges of the Commonwealth Air Forces surrounding the badge of the Royal Air Force. The New Zealand badge is on the lower right of the circle while the New Zealand fern is echoed out all on its own in the lower left hand corner of the outer square. Above the rosette are the words *Per Ardua Ad Astra* ("Through Difficulties to the Stars") This is the motto of both the Royal Air Force and the Royal New Zealand Air Force. A little to the right of this rosette and also embedded in the floor are the badges of six R.N.Z.A.F. squadrons and units. There is a plan at the west end of the church, adjacent to the entrance door, which shows the location of each badge.

Now that New Zealand's air force, which contributed to both the nation's security and world peace over 71 years, has been effectively grounded by a government with a greater loyalty to pacifist ideology than to their own country, Saint Clement Danes is one of the few places that commemorates the Royal New Zealand Air Force. May it, like Saint Clement Danes after the War, rise again from its own ashes.

Proceeding along the wide aisle towards the altar one can see the names of former Chiefs of Air Staff including Lord Elworthy of Timaru and Lord

Newall (third from front) who was Governor-General of New Zealand from 1941 to 1946.

On the north and south walls are the Books of Remembrance recording the names of all air force personnel killed during the Second World War including quite a few New Zealanders. The pages of the books are turned each day.

On the wall to the left of the sanctuary are the names of airmen who have been awarded the Victoria Cross. The first name on the list (and the first airman in the world to be awarded one) is William Rhodes-Moorhouse, the grandson of William Barnard Rhodes who arrived at Lyttelton (then called Port Cooper) in 1836. Three years later this pioneer of Canterbury brought forty breeding cattle from Sydney and established a cattle station at Akaroa; this was the first cattle or sheep farm in the South Island. He later owned the Levels sheep run in South Canterbury where he and his brothers carried more than 100,000 sheep. After he died his daughter moved to England and married Edward Moorhouse. Their son won his Victoria Cross on 26th April, 1915, when he successfully bombed a vital enemy rail junction near Courtrai in Belgium. He crossed the trenches, with their constant anti-aircraft fire, and dropped his bombs. Having satisfied himself that they had done their work, he turned for home. It was then that his plane was attacked by ground fire and a piece of shrapnel struck him. Mortally wounded in the stomach, arms and legs, he flew his BE-2b biplane back to his base and died the next day.

At the time of his death this daredevil pilot had a baby son, William. He too joined the R.A.F and became a pilot but was killed in the Battle of Britain. These two descendants of Canterbury's first farming settler are buried side by side in the grounds of Parnham House, near Bridport, Dorset.

Also on the list of Victoria Cross winners is Sergeant James Ward from Wanganui, a pilot in Bomber Command. On 7th July, 1941, he was returning from a raid over Munster in Germany when his Wellington bomber was attacked by a German fighter plane. Fire broke out in the Wellington's starboard engine and threatened to engulf the whole plane. To save the lives of the crew Ward climbed out and, making foot and hand holes in the wing fabric, successfully smothered the flames with an engine cover. He had to battle terrific winds to get back inside but the plane returned safely to base. A month after receiving his Victoria Cross he was killed during a bombing raid over Germany.

Another New Zealander on the board is Nelson born Squadron Leader Trent, also of Bomber Command, who won his award for conspicuous bravery during a raid over Amsterdam on 3rd May, 1943.

This daylight attack on the heavily defended Amsterdam Power Station was met by an overwhelming force of Messerschmitts as soon as the R.A.F. Venturas reached the Dutch coast. Although six Venturas were shot down Squadron Leader Trent flew on through murderous fire and dropped his bombs on the target. Almost immediately his plane was shot down; two of his aircrew were killed but he and the navigator survived and became prisoners-of-war in Stalag Luft III.

Further down is the name of Flying Officer Lloyd Allen Trigg who was born at Houhora, North Auckland, in 1914. He received the V.C. posthumously after his aircraft caught on fire during an attack on a German U-boat on 11th August, 1943. Because of the threat that the U-boats posed to the Atlantic convoys, which literally kept Britain alive, the destruction of the U-boats was a priority where the pilots took even greater risks than usual.

Across the aisle from the pulpit is the McIndoe seat which is where the crucifier (the man carrying the cross) sits during services. The seat was given in memory of the Dunedin born plastic surgeon, Sir Archibald McIndoe, by the Guinea Pig Club which was an association formed by those airmen whose faces and bodies were restored at McIndoe's hospital at East Grinstead in Sussex. A feature of the seat is the flying pig crest. (See: East Grinstead, Sussex)

From the altar one can look back and see two colourful banners hanging over the balcony. The one on the right (looking from the altar) is the Garter banner of Lord Elworthy. The Garter, the highest order of English knighthood, is in the personal gift of the Sovereign; therefore, it is not "politically tainted" as is the case with so many other honours.

When a man is elevated to the Garter he has his own stall in Saint George's Chapel, Windsor, over which hangs his personal banner. Upon his death the banner is taken down and given to his family. When this was done in the case of Lord Elworthy his family presented it to Saint Clement Danes in recognition of his long and distinguished career in the Royal Air Force. The other banner is that of Lord Portal, Chief of Air Staff during the Second World War, which was presented by his family in similar circumstances.

On 12th September, 1975, a memorial service was held in this church for the greatest of all New Zealanders, Sir Keith Park who, as commander of Number 11 Group in the Battle of Britain, had tactical command of the entire battle. In the words of Lord Tedder, former British chief of air staff, "If ever any one man won the Battle of Britain, he (Park) did. I don't believe it is realised how much one man, with his leadership, his calm judgement and his skill, did to save not only this country but also the world."

Sir Keith Park was born in Thames, New Zealand in 1892. He joined the Territorial Army in 1911. Upon the outbreak of the First World War he went overseas with the New Zealand Expeditionary Force and saw action in both Gallipoli and France. In 1917 he transferred to the Royal Flying Corps and was awarded the Military Cross (twice), the French Croix de Guerre and the Distinguished Flying Cross. He joined the Royal Air Force when it was formed in 1918 and eventually became one of its greatest commanders. After he retired he settled in Remuera, Auckland, and served on the Auckland City Council. At his memorial service here at Saint Clement's the eulogy was delivered by the legless war ace, Douglas Bader, who concluded his address with the words, "British military history of this century has been enriched with the names of great fighting men from New Zealand, of all ranks and in every one of our services. Keith Park's name is carved into that history alongside those of his peers."

Before leaving this ancient and beautiful church, which has the names of so many New Zealand pilots recorded in its Books of Remembrance, don't forget to sign the Visitors' Book.

Outside the front of the church (facing towards Australia House) is a statue of William Ewart Gladstone, five times Prime Minister of Great Britain, after whom the Wairarapa town of Gladstone is named as well as the main street of Gisborne. He was a powerful friend of the Canterbury Association which was responsible for founding the province of Canterbury. As Colonial Secretary he overturned Governor Fitzroy's revocation of Commissioner Spain's award of 60,000 acres of Taranaki to the New Zealand Company, thereby enabling the settlers to expand beyond the narrow confines of New Plymouth.

Continuing along the Strand towards Fleet Street one can see on the right the little lanes that lead down to the Georgian brick buildings and neat gardens of the Temple. There are four Inns of Court – Inner Temple, Middle Temple, Lincoln's Inn and Gray's Inn. These ancient societies have the exclusive right of calling people to the Bar of England and Wales and every barrister must be a member of one of them. The Inns are rich colleges dating from the Middle Ages and their extensive and well-kept gardens provide a haven of tranquillity in the heart of London.

Over the years several prominent New Zealanders have been members of the Inns of Court starting with Sir William Fox, four times Prime Minister of New Zealand in the nineteenth century, after whom Fox Glacier was named. He emigrated to New Zealand in 1842 only six weeks after being called to the Bar in Inner Temple Hall. In 1906 New Zealand's greatest tennis player, Anthony Wilding, also donned his black gown for the same purpose as did Lord Cooke of Thorndon, the former President of the New Zealand Court of Appeal, in 1954.

Each Inn is run by its Benchers who are usually senior judges, leading barristers and eminent professors of law. Sir Thaddeus McCarthy, another former President of the New Zealand Court of Appeal, was an Honorary Bencher of the Middle Temple. William Sefton Moorhouse, an early Superintendent of Canterbury, was a Middle Temple barrister who practised for three years before sailing out to New Zealand.

So too was C.W.Richmond, a pioneer of New Plymouth, Native Minister and Supreme Court judge. Another Middle Templar was Alfred Domett, who became Premier of New Zealand in 1862. He created the Native Land Courts and, being a literary man, built up the General Assembly Library at Parliament. He also wrote *Ranolf and Amohia*, a 14,000 line epic poem about a Maori maiden and Ranolf the Englishman.

Definitely the most literate man ever to be Prime Minister.

One of the oldest and most interesting buildings in the Temple is the round shaped Temple Church which dates back to the Crusades. It is one of only five round churches in Britain and was built in imitation of the Church of the Holy Sepulchre at Jerusalem. The round nave was consecrated in 1185 and the chancel was added half a century later. Of this church the New Zealand author, Alan Mulgan, wrote, "I thought it more flawless than any church in London or perhaps in England…..The recumbent figures of knights under the dome are completely in keeping with their surroundings." It was in this church that Lord Bledisloe, Governor-General of New Zealand from 1929 to 1934, was married on 17th December, 1898. His wife later died and he subsequently remarried. Bledisloe was a barrister of the Inner Temple and that was why he was allowed to be married in the historic Temple church, which is the church for both Inner and Middle Temple.

Lord Bledisloe was one of the most popular and respected Governors that New Zealand ever had. In 1931 he presented the Bledisloe Cup for rugby competition between Australia and New Zealand.

The following year he purchased the property where the Treaty of Waitangi was signed in 1840 – including James Busby's house (now known as the Treaty House) and a thousand acres of adjoining land. He presented all this to New Zealand as a national memorial and the first ceremony was held there on the anniversary of the signing of the Treaty on 6th February, 1934.

The point at which the Strand becomes Fleet Street is marked by a statue in the middle of the road which marks the boundary between the city of Westminster and the City of London. Whenever the Queen makes a ceremonial entry to the City of London she is met here by the Lord Mayor. In accordance with ancient custom he tenders the sword of state, which the Sovereign then returns to him and she then enters his bailwick.

The road on the left is Chancery Lane which leads to High Holborn. On the north side of High Holborn is the arched entrance to Gray's Inn, another of the Inns of Court which has many links with New Zealand.

Sir Denis Blundell, former Governor-General of New Zealand, was called to the Bar of Gray's Inn in 1929. Another former Governor-General, Sir David Beattie, was an Honorary Bencher of Gray's Inn as were former Prime Minister, Sir John Marshall and President of the Court of Appeal, Sir Alfred North.

Edward Gibbon Wakefield (1796-1862), who did so much to promote the successful colonisation of New Zealand, became a member of Gray's Inn on 5th October, 1813. Wakefield was of Quaker stock and his father was a cousin of Elizabeth Fry, the famous prison reformer. His uncle Daniel was a barrister and the young Edward joined Gray's Inn with the intention of entering the legal profession. It was fortunate for New Zealand that he didn't.

In 1827 Wakefield was convicted at Lancaster Assizes of abduction and was imprisoned for three years. His great imagination, humane values and perseverance in face of difficulties provided the motor that powered his colonising efforts which enabled the New Zealand settlements to develop as free and well-balanced communities, untainted by the convict element of most of the Australian colonies.

Returning along Chancery Lane to Fleet Street and continuing along that thoroughfare in an easterly direction, one will see the steeple of Saint Bride's church on the right. This church, which was bombed during the Second World War and has now been restored, has a sister church at Waiuku in New Zealand. The New Zealand church has a stained glass window which depicts the steeple of Saint Bride's, London, the only part of the structure to survive the bombing. Perhaps the most interesting result of the bombing was that it revealed catacombs that nobody knew about.

Crossing Farringdon Road and proceeding up the gentle slope of Ludgate Hill one sees a street on the left which is known as Old Bailey, famous for its Central Criminal Court where Britain's most notorious felons have been tried – from Doctor Crippen to the Yorkshire Ripper and I.R.A. terrorists. Panelling from the court, known colloquially as "the Old Bailey", forms part of Courtroom No. 1 of the High Court in Wellington. And not far from Wellington's High Court is the Old Bailey pub in Lambton Quay.

Continuing up Ludgate Hill we reach Saint

Paul's Cathedral which is regarded as the parish church of the British Commonwealth.

Most cathedrals took centuries to build but Sir Christopher Wren, the architect of Saint Paul's, lived to see the completion of his masterpiece which was only thirty-six years in the making. He used to tie himself into a chair which was then hoisted up on a pulley to the dome where he would give directions to the craftsmen.

During the Second World War the area around Saint Paul's was destroyed by enemy bombing but the great cathedral suffered only relatively minor damage – mostly to the North Transept. At the time it was widely believed that its survival was the work of God but the vigilance of its firewatchers, who stood guard every night, also had something to do with it. A major restoration of the cathedral was carried out in the 1970s to which New Zealand contributed £50,000.

In the 1960s New Zealander, Venerable Martin Sullivan of Christchurch, was Archdeacon of London and Canon in residence at Saint Paul's. In this capacity he read the Lesson at the state funeral of Sir Winston Churchill in January, 1965. On this sad yet magnificent occasion Ven. Sullivan led the Earl Marshal's procession from the great West Doors (the cathedral entrance) to the altar. Behind him came the heralds, then the pall-bearers and finally the coffin itself. "It was the greatest and proudest moment of my life", he said.

In the apse of the Cathedral (behind the altar) is the American Memorial Chapel, the windows of which were designed by the British artist, Brian Thomas, who also created the six great windows in the Nave of the new Saint Paul's Cathedral in Wellington.

Several people who had associations with the founding of New Zealand and the naming of its cities are buried in Saint Paul's.

On 26th September, 1898, the funeral took place here of Sir George Grey, the capable and energetic autocrat who had been both Governor and Premier of New Zealand and who built a beautiful home on Kawau Island in the Hauraki Gulf. Grey donated his collection of rare books, paintings, manuscripts and Maori artefacts to the Auckland Public Library. Greymouth and Greytown in New Zealand are named after him as well as the Auckland suburb of Grey Lynn. Sir George Grey is buried here in the Crypt. Above his tomb is a marble bust of him that was erected by the Government and people of New Zealand.

Also in the Crypt is a bas-relief of Richard John Seddon, the West Coaster who was Prime Minister of New Zealand from 1893 to 1906. Seddon was a disciple of Grey's and between them they had an enormous influence on New Zealand's history at a particularly important point.

There is also a memorial plaque to those who fell at Gallipoli and on Anzac Day each year a memorial service is held here at 9.30 a.m.

Grey's funeral did not match that of the Duke of Wellington after whom New Zealand's capital city is named. One and a half million people watched the funeral procession of the great Duke and he is buried here along with Nelson, who also gave his famous name to New Zealand's sunniest city. In the words of the New Zealand writer, Alan Mulgan, "Nelson and Wellington lie here, and the man whose emotions do not warm to these names is wasting his time going down to the Crypt."

Not far from the Duke of Wellington is the resting place of General Picton, who was second-in-command at Waterloo until he fell heroically on the battlefield. Just as the two men were linked by the chain of command at Waterloo and are buried only a few feet away from each other, so too are their names indelibly linked in New Zealand with the ferries between the North and South Islands plying between Picton and Wellington.

Nelson's coffin was made from the mainmast of the French ship, *L'Orient,* and it is enclosed in a sarcophagus of black and white marble. Not far from Nelson lies Admiral Collingwood (1750-1810) who assumed command of the British fleet at Trafalgar when Nelson died and in whose honour the town of Collingwood, near Nelson in New Zealand, is named.

There is also a statue of the Napier brothers, Charles and William, which can be seen south of the Nelson chamber in the Crypt. The city of Napier in the Hawkes Bay was named after the former. (See: Trafalgar Square)

There are also memorials to Lord Freyberg V.C. (1889-1963), commander of the New Zealand Division in the Second World War and Governor-General, and to another Governor-General, Admiral Jellicoe.

Probably the most interesting grave in the cathedral is that of Wren himself. He lies under the Choir, the words on his tomb being *Si monumentum requiris, circumspice.* ("If you want his memorial, look around you.")

Saint Paul's was the setting for the wedding of the Prince of Wales and Diana in 1981, when New Zealand's gift to the singing world, Kiri Te Kanawa, filled Wren's cathedral with her beautiful voice. She sang her aria from the North Transept.

Also in the North Transept is the memorial to the 57th (West Middlesex) Regiment which served in the Taranaki during the Maori War of the 1860s. Known as the "Die Hards", they were involved in several skirmishes against the Hauhaus and others.

Among the names listed is that of Ensign John Down V.C. An old boy of prestigious Westminster School, Ensign Down won the Victoria Cross for gallantry during an action in 1863 at Allan's Hill, five and a half miles out of New Plymouth on the south road when, under fire from the nearby bush, he went to the rescue of a mortally wounded comrade.

On Sunday, 1st September, 1850, a special service was held in Saint Paul's for the colonists of the First Four Ships who were about to sail to New Zealand to found the settlement of Canterbury. The Archbishop of Canterbury, Doctor Sumner, preached the sermon and gave his special blessing to the undertaking. The result of this divine invocation was that Canterbury quickly developed into the most successful settlement that the British ever made abroad. In July, 2000, there was a special service in Saint Paul's to commemorate Canterbury's 150th anniversary and once again the Archbishop of Canterbury gave the sermon.

There is a piece of Saint Paul's in New Zealand. Sir Heaton Rhodes was a large landholder in Canterbury and Minister of Defence for New Zealand 1920-6. He created Otahuna, one of New Zealand's most beautiful gardens, for his wife, Jessie; when she died he built a small church in her memory at Tai Tapu, south of Christchurch. It was designed by Cecil Wood and was consecrated in 1932. One wall of this lovely country church incorporates a stone from Saint Paul's cathedral in London.

A further link with Canterbury is that the ten bells of Christchurch Cathedral are duplicates of the upper ten bells of Saint Paul's in London.

Proceeding along Cheapside in an easterly direction from Saint Paul's Underground station, turn left up King Street to the Guildhall, which is the "town hall" of the City of London. More than five hundred years ago Dick Whittington, the famous Lord Mayor of London, helped to build it.

When the dominion prime ministers were in London for important meetings prior to the D-Day landings the Prime Minister of New Zealand, Peter Fraser, was given the Freedom of the City of London at a ceremony in the Guildhall.

With the Lord Mayor of London in his gold and black gown presiding and the aldermen in their scarlet robes this was an ancient ceremony of great splendour but with a difference; there was a bare iron roof to replace the oaken rafters that had been destroyed by the Luftwaffe and some of the statues in the hall had lost their arms and legs to the bombs.

Peter Fraser, accompanied by his wife, Thames (N.Z.) born Air Vice-Marshal Park (See: Saint Clement Danes church, London) and the other Prime Ministers, signed the parchment in the traditional words that he would "pay his scot and bear his lot". Hitler could do his worst but the timeless rituals of England could not be stamped out. It is in times of stress that traditions and ancient institutions prove their worth by providing symbols of strength and unity.

After emerging from the Guildhall at the end of the ceremony Peter Fraser looked at the bomb damage all around him for this, the heart of the city, was one of the worst hit areas. A local remarked, "You certainly are seeing London at its worst", to which Fraser replied, "Yes, I see the city at its worst, but the people at their best."

The Guildhall has now been restored – partly with a gift in 1957 of £3,500 from the Municipal Association of New Zealand for the purchase of timber.

Among the many ceremonies that take place in the restored Guildhall is the award of the Booker Prize for fiction; this is regarded as the most prestigious literary prize in the English speaking world. It was here at the Guildhall that New Zealand authoress, Keri Hulme, was awarded the Booker in 1985 for her novel, *The Bone People*.

The interesting thing about *The Bone People* was that it was rejected by virtually every publisher in

New Zealand so plucky Keri published it herself with the help of a few friends. Result: the largest ever sales for a New Zealand written novel and some very red faces in the publishing industry. For those who want to see inside the Guildhall it is open to the public during normal business hours.

Part of the destruction that caught Fraser's eye were the ruins of the church of Saint Lawrence Jewry in front of the Guildhall.

The original church, built in 1136, was burnt down in the Great Fire of London in 1666 and was replaced eleven years later by a fine new structure that was built by Sir Christopher Wren, the architect of Saint Paul's. The reason why Wren designed so many churches was that he was the leading architect of the period following the Great Fire when so many churches were burned down and had to be rebuilt. Astronomer, mathematician, architect and administrator, this "man for all seasons" proved himself more than equal to the task.

Sadly Wren's lovely structure was destroyed by German incendiary bombs on the night of 29th December, 1940, in the fire bomb raid on this part of the City. Only the shell of the building was left standing.

The present church, which rose on the ashes of the old, was finished in 1957. With its fine Corinthian columns, square tower and ornamental ceiling, it is almost an exact replica of Wren's design. In the vestibule by the North Entrance is a glass cupboard where relics of the earlier church can be seen.

Because of its proximity to the Guildhall Saint Lawrence Jewry is the official church of the City of London, the Lord Mayor's pew being at the front on the right hand side of the aisle.

It is also the church of the New Zealand Society in London and every year New Zealand's national day is commemorated here with a church service which is usually followed by a reception put on by the Worshipful Company of Girdlers in Girdlers' Hall. The Girdlers is one of the ancient livery companies of the City of London that have grown out of the mediaeval guilds for different occupations. The Girdlers' Company sponsors four scholarships each year for New Zealand students to attend Corpus Christi College, Oxford.

The side chapel, known as the Commonwealth Chapel, is separated from the Nave by a carved oak screen. The name of the Chapel commemorates the role played in the development of the British Empire and Commonwealth by the City of London. It was not until the 1950s that New Zealand developed a capital market and the funds for its pioneer projects like the South Island's Midland Railway and the building of the Auckland tramway system would never have proceeded but for the finance provided by the City of London.

The coats-of-arms of the Commonwealth countries, including New Zealand's, can be seen in the stained glass windows on either side of the Saint George window while the New Zealand flag is also on display. The window depicting Christ's Ascension into Heaven was given by the Auckland Power Board. Its lower section shows the sadness of the Crucifixion, which is intended to be a contrast with the triumph of the Ascension.

The curious name of this church is first, in honour of the third century saint who suffered martyrdom on a gridiron and secondly, a reminder that this area was inhabited by Jews until they were expelled from the kingdom by King Edward I in 1290.

Saint Lawrence Jewry is open on week-days from 7.30 a.m. to 2 p.m. There is a service at 8.30 a.m. on Wednesdays and 1.15 p.m. on Fridays.

From Bank station it is a one stop ride on the District or Circle Line to Tower Hill, the stop for the Tower of London, Britain's most popular tourist destination.

On Tower Hill is the Tower Hill Memorial which commemorates 36,550 members of the Merchant Navy and fishing fleets who were killed at sea during the two world wars and who have no known grave other than the ocean deep.

Among those commemorated are thirty-six New Zealanders, including two sixteen year olds, Cadets John Proudfoot of Queenstown and William Shaw of Dunollie on the West Coast, both drowning within four days of each other as a result of separate attacks by enemy submarines.

THE EAST END

"Not a wery nice neighbourhood this, Sir," said Sam.
"It is not indeed, " replied Mr. Pickwick.

> - Description of Whitechapel in *Pickwick Papers* by Charles Dickens.

London has always been divided into two parts; west of the City is the fashionable "West End" while the area to the east is the "East End" which has traditionally been the home of the Cockneys. Each went their separate ways and even to-day there are old people who have lived in the East End all their lives without ever having been to the West End and vice versa.

The East End was centred around the docks in the age before the aeroplane when Britain was mistress of the world's seas. However, as a result of the bombing by the Luftwaffe, the moving of shipping down to the container port at Tilbury and the influx of large numbers of Bengalis and other foreigners into the area, the character of the East End has changed beyond all recognition.

For New Zealanders the East End is of interest for two reasons: from its now disused docks many of the sailing ships departed for New Zealand with the early settlers and it was in the East End that Captain Cook lived after he left Yorkshire.

We shall begin our "Cook's tour" of the East End by taking a District Line tube to Whitechapel. On the pavement outside the station there is usually a busy street market. Turn left and walk past the Blind Beggar pub and into Mile End Road. When you see the bust of King Edward VII on the grass verge between the pavement and the road, cross to the other side which is now a post-war housing estate. At the (east) end of the housing estate is an old brick wall (No. 88). It was in a house on this site that Captain Cook lived between 1764 and 1776. Cook bought the property shortly after his first son was born and he lived here until he left on his last fatal voyage from which he never returned.

During the years that he was based in London Cook always lived in the East End because it was near the docks where his various ships were berthed. This house was a respectable distance from the river; in general, the closer an area was to the river, the more disreputable it was. Behind Cook's house was a garden where Mrs. Cook could take the air and the captain could sit in the summer months, writing up his famous journals and playing games with his sons.

Even in those days the Mile End Road was a busy thoroughfare with coaches rattling along it on their way from the City to different parts of Essex. Nearby were some fields where, after Cook's return from his first voyage to the Pacific, he grazed the first animal ever to travel from New Zealand to England; this was a goat that Cook took around the world with him on the *Endeavour* to provide fresh milk for the crew. At the places where he landed in New Zealand it would be tethered to a tree to feed on some fresh grass – the precursor of the millions of sheep and cattle that were later to graze on New Zealand's prolific grasslands to provide meat for the people of Britain.

It was also in this house that Mrs. Cook learned the terrible news of her husband's gory death in the Hawaiian islands. On the wall is a black plaque recording Captain Cook's residence here and stating, "In three voyages he charted the coasts of New Zealand, the coast of Australia and the Pacific coast of North America".

Of even greater interest in the Captain Cook story is Saint Margaret's, Barking, for it was here that he got married on 21st December, 1762.

Barking is reached on the District Line and is nine stops east of Whitechapel. Turn right outside the station, go past the band rotunda and then along East Street where there is a thriving market every Tuesday, Thursday and Saturday. At the end of the street is the ancient church of Saint Margaret's where the discoverer of New Zealand walked down the aisle in his naval uniform to take locally born Elizabeth Batts as his lawfully wedded wife.

On the day Cook, aged thirty-four, and his twenty-one year old bride walked together over the meadows in order to reach the church. Their marriage was by licence of the Archbishop of Canterbury which meant that they did not have to wait for the calling of banns. Having made up his mind to get married, Cook, always a man of decision, was not prepared to wait.

After the service the newly-weds went by river to Cook's lodgings in Shadwell where they lived together until the following April when the bridegroom returned to the sea to survey the coast of Newfoundland.

The stone church of Saint Margaret's stands among the ruins of Barking Abbey which was founded in 666 A.D. by a Saxon lord, Erkenwald, who later became Bishop of London. Ransacked by the Vikings, it was rebuilt in 970. William the Conqueror lived there while he was waiting for the Tower of London to be built.

The Abbey was closed by Henry VIII in 1539 as part of the Dissolution of the Monasteries but the church survived as Barking's parish church. The oldest part of the church is the chancel which was built in the early thirteenth century; parts of the south wall and the north arcade also date from this time. The tower was built in the late 1400s and the rest of the church was finished a century later.

Next to the church is Saint Margaret's Centre which is open Monday-Friday, 10 a.m.-2 p.m., Saturdays 10-noon and Sundays 8.30-noon. During these times the church is open and it is possible to buy Captain Cook's family tree and a copy of the entry in the registry of his marriage, which is in fine copperplate script. The original is no longer kept in the church since all parish records have been transferred to central registries. The original marriage entry is at Chelmsford Records Office.

What an ideal church for a New Zealander to get married in – to walk down the same aisle and for the same purpose as Captain Cook in a church that remains unchanged since 1762. Non-parishioners can have their

Captain Cook's marriage certificate.
Copies can be purchased at Saint Margaret's, Barking, the church where the discoverer of New Zealand was married on 21st December, 1762. The church is unchanged since Cook walked down the aisle.

weddings at Saint Margaret's if they get a special licence from the bishop. The vicar can be contacted at Saint Margaret's Centre, Tel. 8594-2932 (mornings).

SOUTH LONDON

"The greatest genius that perhaps human nature has yet produced"

Samuel Taylor Coleridge on Shakespeare

In Tudor times the south bank of the Thames, opposite the City of London, was an entertainment area and in 1599 the Globe Theatre, a small and lofty circular structure open to the sky, was established in Park Street near the point where the present Southwark Bridge reaches the South Bank or, as it is still sometimes called, the Surrey side of the river.

Shakespeare was a shareholder in the Globe. Not only did he act on its stage but also fifteen of his plays were produced there. Unfortunately the theatre burned down in 1613 but was rebuilt with a tiled roof. This second Globe was closed down by the Puritans in 1642 and that was the end of this cradle of Shakespearean drama for the next three centuries.

When American actor, Sam Wannamaker, arrived in London in 1949 he made his way to Southwark to seek out the site of the old Globe. All he could find was a small plaque to mark the site. This imaginative and enterprising gentleman had a vision of making this hallowed spot into a more fitting memorial to the greatest writer of the English language whose plays used to thrill the rowdy Elizabethan audiences. It took decades for his dream to become reality and sadly Wannaker did not live to see it as he died in 1993. It is indeed appropriate that an American should have brought it into being since Shakespeare is the common property of the entire English speaking world. It was in this spirit that the Wellington Shakespeare Society in New Zealand decided to initiate the project to create the stage hangings as its contribution to the resurrection of the Globe.

Designed by Raymond Boyce and overseen by Dawn Sanders more than 500 embroiderers, quilters and textile artists – most of them members of the Association of New Zealand Embroiderers' Guilds – undertook the mammoth task. It took them sixteen months; they started at the beginning of 1990 and finished on 23rd April, 1991, which was Shakespeare's birthday. During this time Sam Wannamaker visited New Zealand to view the work in progress. Altogether they used more than two hundred yards of fabric as well as several miles of thread.

In Shakespeare's time there was very little stage scenery, the Bard preferring to let his language provoke the imagination. Since there were no relics or records of what a Shakespearean stage hanging looked like the embroiderers had to be somewhat inventive. One of the four hangings shows the figure of Atlas holding up a globe of the world with little New Zealand prominently portrayed even though in Shakespeare's day it was an unknown land. This is a suitable symptom of

Tapestry at the Globe Theatre, London
Photograph: Julia Brooke-White
This magnificent tapestry of Atlas holding up a globe of the world was woven by more than 500 embroiderers, quilters and textile artists in New Zealand. One of four stage hangings, it was presented to the Globe by the Wellington Shakespeare Society.

Shakespeare's works – they are for all people for all time.

The other hangings are of Hercules and Venus and Adonis. Young Adonis is seen spurning the advances of Venus who plots her revenge. The next day the beautiful young man rides out to hunt and is gored to death by a boar.

When they were completed the hangings were displayed throughout New Zealand, Australia, the United States and Canada and were viewed by more than a million people.

They provided the background to the stage on 12th June, 1997, when a special production, *Triumphs and Mirths*, was staged at the Royal Opening Performance in the presence of the Queen.

The hangings are used only on special occasions and are normally on display in the vast gallery beneath the theatre which is known as "Underglobe" – a word that is taken from *King Lear*. No New Zealander could view these wonderful creations without feeling a surge of pride. Already they stand with the Bayeux Tapestry and the beautiful hanging in Coventry Cathedral as among the most famous works of embroidery in the world.

Upon entering the Globe theatre on a specially conducted tour (strongly recommended) one walks over a court of paving stones which were donated by various people and organisations – including ones from New Plymouth Boys' High School, Christchurch Girls' High School and the Shakespeare Globe Centre in New Zealand.

The new Globe, with its thatched roof, whitewashed Tudor style walls and distinctive circular shape, was opened in 1995 and holds 1,500 people for Shakespearean performances under open skies and in natural light. It is as close a replica as possible to its Elizabethan predecessor even to the extent of unseasoned oak being used for the timber framing, the boards being wedged together without nuts or bolts.

There is also a permanent exhibition on the theatre of the sixteenth and seventeenth centuries. In Underglobe can be seen a reproduction of an Elizabethan tiring room (the room above the stage) and it is possible to try on armour and see all the yards of cloth that were needed to make a single ruff.

Situated at 21 New Globe Walk at Bankside, the recreated playhouse is open daily from May to September, 9 a.m. to midday for Exhibition and theatre tours. From October to April the opening hours are 10 a.m. to 5 p.m. Tel: 020-7902-1500. For box office bookings telephone 020-7401-9919. The season for watching plays is the same as in Shakespeare's time – May to September.

Another place on the South Bank of interest to New Zealanders is the Imperial War Museum in Lambeth Road, south of Waterloo Station. The nearest Underground station is Lambeth North.

There are several exhibits of campaigns in which New Zealand soldiers have fought including Gallipoli and the Battle of Britain. Among the displays is the head dress worn by a New Zealand soldier during the Middle East campaign of the Second World War.

WHITEHALL AND WESTMINSTER

"Think how many royal bones
Sleep within these heaps of stones!"

> - Francis Beaumont, *On the Tombs in Westminster Abbey*

From the lower end of Trafalgar Square the Houses of Parliament and Big Ben can be seen at the end of the road known as Whitehall, which is lined on both sides by government offices. Half way down on the left is the Ministry of Defence building with four statues on its lawn. The last of these is the familiar figure of Field-Marshal Montgomery, under whose overall command the New Zealand Division fought to victory over Rommel in North Africa in 1942. Monty is wearing his famous beret; in fact, when he died, the only item on his coffin was the black beret.

On the other side of Whitehall are the large iron gates that lead to Downing Street, the home of the British Prime Minister. The gates were erected in the 1980s at the height of the I.R.A. terrorist campaign against both prominent figures and ordinary members of the public. Before that one was free to walk along Downing Street, stand outside the famous door of Number Ten and have one's picture taken.

However, for New Zealanders No. 6 Downing Street is just as important as the famous Number Ten for it is here in a small, oak panelled room that the Judicial Committee of the Privy Council (New Zealand's highest and oldest court) hears its cases.

The Privy Council was formerly the inner council of officials who in the Middle Ages attended to the King's business. It became convenient for it to function through committees; one of these evolved into the Cabinet while another continues as the Judicial Committee and it is this latter that has always served as New Zealand's highest court. Senior law lords sit on the Judicial Committee; most of them are English but they are sometimes joined by a senior New Zealand judge who derives considerable benefit out of sitting on a panel of such eminent jurists.

Technically the Judicial Committee of the Privy Council is not a court; it simply hears appeals and then tenders its advice to the Queen who, by convention, confirms its findings at a meeting of the wider Privy Council at Buckingham Palace, thereby personifying the ancient role of the Sovereign as the fountain of justice. By tradition the Prime Minister, senior Cabinet Ministers and Leader of the Opposition of Britain and New Zealand and other dominions are Privy Counsellors as well as senior judges and other high office holders like the Lord Chamberlain and the Queen's Private Secretary.

Ever since its founding in 1840 New Zealand has derived considerable benefit out of having this Committee of the Privy Council, consisting of some of the most eminent judges of the English speaking world, as its highest court. There is an old adage that justice should be blind and in a small country like New Zealand there is a danger that judges either consciously or unconsciously might be influenced by certain powerful interests and so it is important to have as our highest court something as distant and objective as the Judicial Committee of the Privy Council which, away from the heat of local controversy, can decide issues in a cool, honest and rational manner. To their lordships in London, parties to proceedings are only names on a piece of paper and so justice is more likely to be done. And, of course, with "double dipping", travel expense "irregularities", the bias of the Family Court and judges being appointed for reasons of political correctness rather than their ability, the honesty and integrity of the New Zealand judiciary in recent times leave quite a lot to be desired. Hence the importance of this wise and ancient court, with a pedigree going back to the Middle Ages, as the ultimate guarantor of our rights and liberties.

The building on the corner of Downing Street and Whitehall (the corner nearest Parliament Square) is the graceful structure that used to house the Colonial Office from which New Zealand was governed in the nineteenth century. Since there is no longer a British Empire it is now part of that bureaucratic monstrosity that calls itself the Foreign Office.

It is interesting to note that in the nineteenth century both the Colonial Office and the India Office and other government departments were housed in this building. In other words from a few rooms here in Whitehall less than a hundred officials governed the whole British Empire which embraced one quarter of mankind. Compare this with the present occupant, the Foreign Office, which fills this and other buildings with countless bureaucrats who are performing a much lesser function as Britain surrenders more and more of its ancient and hard fought for sovereignty to undemocratic E.U. institutions.

A few yards past the entrance to Downing Street and in the middle of the road is the Cenotaph, described by the New Zealand writer, Alan Mulgan, as follows: "In beauty, simplicity and dignity it is the ideal war memorial". On Anzac Day each year a wreath laying ceremony takes place at 11 a.m. The British, of course, have their own day of commemoration on 11th November, the anniversary of the Armistice that ended the First World War. The tradition is for men to raise their hats as they pass this sacred spot.

The next street on the right is King Charles Street at the end of which is a fine statue of Robert Clive (1725-74) after whom the Hawkes Bay town of Clive was named. Arriving in India at the age of eighteen as a clerk in the East India Company, Clive's abilities were soon recognised by his superiors. When the French attacked Madras in 1746 Clive was transferred to military duties. His subsequent victories at Arcot and Plassey (1757) made the British the masters of Bengal and, since Bengal was the key to India, the masters of the whole sub-continent.

It was believed by Alfred Domett, the Commissioner of Crown Lands and Resident Magistrate at Ahuriri in 1854, that Clive would become the main town of the Hawkes Bay while Napier would be its subsidiary port (like Christchurch and Lyttelton). At the time Hawkes Bay was part of Wellington Province and Domett wrote to the Superintendent of Wellington, "almost all the inhabitants of this district united….that the principal town might be called after the great founder of our Indian Empire, Lord Clive, and as it appears that the port town can only be subordinate, I would propose that the latter be named in commemoration of one of our greatest and best Indian Captains just dead – Sir Charles Napier". Domett's prediction that Napier would be nothing more than the port for the great city of Clive was not to be fulfilled.

At the end of Whitehall are the impressive buildings of the Houses of Parliament with Big Ben chiming the hour.

Since this is the "Mother of Parliaments" and the home of our own "Westminster system of government", it is only natural that New Zealanders should have an interest in the history of parliamentary government on this historic site.

The original Palace of Westminster had been built by King Edward the Confessor. When William the Conqueror arrived from Normandy in 1066 he did not like the place as he had been used to the grander palaces of France. He rebuilt it and in 1097 his son, William Rufus (William II), added Westminster Hall.

It was in this magnificent Hall that the trial took place on 23rd August, 1305, of William Wallace, the Scottish rebel whose story was made into the film *Braveheart* with the usual Hollywood distortion of history. The spot where Wallace stood during his short trial can still be seen. Other famous trials that have taken place in Westminster Hall were those of Guy Fawkes, King Charles I and Warren Hastings, after whom the Hawkes Bay city of Hastings is named (See: Daylesford, Gloucestershire). This ancient and historic structure has one of the finest hammer beam roofs in Europe, the oak beams rising to a height of 90 feet at the centre of the Gothic arches. On 17th June, 1974, Irish Republican Army arsonists set fire to Westminster Hall. It burned for three and a half hours and injured twenty people. This was a deliberate attempt to strike at something that was of symbolic importance to all the English speaking peoples whose liberties derive from events that took place in this building. The Hall has now been restored.

Westminster Hall was the site of England's first Parliament in 1265 when King Henry III's barons, knights and subjects forced him to reform his government to include representatives of the people.

This Parliament was largely the work of Simon de Montfort, the brother-in-law of the King, who is widely regarded as the founder of representative government for the Anglo-Saxon world. The Parliament that he summoned to meet here at Westminster on 20th January, 1265, contained not only two knights from each shire but also two citizens from each city and two burgesses elected by each borough. This was the first time that those other than knights and barons had been summoned to a Parliament. The ordinary people now had their voice in the affairs of the kingdom. Parliamentary representation, which has always been the lynchpin of New Zealand democracy, can be traced all the way back to this ground breaking Parliament here at Westminster in the winter of 1265.

In the House of Commons the two elaborate dispatch boxes, mounted with bronze, were donated by New Zealand after the Second World War as the old ones were lost when the Commons debating chamber was destroyed by fire in an air raid on 10th May, 1941. When Churchill visited the bombed and still smouldering chamber he wept and vowed that it would be rebuilt exactly as it had been. And it was. At the entrance to the restored House of Commons is the Churchill Arch, which is constructed from stone that was salvaged from the bombed chamber.

For the rest of the War the Members of the House of Commons had to use the House of Lords as their chamber while the Lords very kindly moved their debates to the Robing Room.

These dispatch boxes contain copies of the Old and New Testaments and the texts of the Oath and Affirmation that are used by Members upon taking their seats for the first time.

It was here in the British Parliament that the New Zealand Constitution Act was passed in 1852. This was the statute which gave responsible government to the settlers, allowing them to run their own affairs instead of being ruled by a British Governor through his council. And it was here that the Statute of Westminster was passed in 1931 which granted full autonomy to New Zealand and the other self-governing dominions "united by common allegiance to the Crown".

Peter Fraser worked as an odd job carpenter at the Houses of Parliament from 1908 to 1910, shortly before he emigrated to New Zealand where he later became Prime Minister. This was a remarkable progress as Members of the House of Commons were not used to seeing their odd job men become Prime Ministers.

At the other end of the building is the House of Lords where several distinguished New Zealanders have sat over the years including the physicist, Lord Rutherford (ex-head boy of Nelson College), Lord Porritt, an old boy of Wanganui Collegiate, Lord Freyberg and Lord Grey of Nuneaton (old boys of Wellington College), Lord Elworthy, who was educated at Marlborough College in England, and, more recently, Lord Cooke of Thorndon, who is also an old boy of Wanganui Collegiate.

As a peer, Lord Rutherford spoke in the House of Lords on only two occasions – both times in support of industrial research. That is one of the features of the House of Lords; their lordships generally speak only on subjects that they know a lot about - unlike in the House of Commons where loud-mouthed know-alls declaim on all sorts of matters of which they have no end of opinions but very little knowledge. Not unlike the New Zealand House of Representatives.

There are regular tours of the chambers of both Houses and of other parts of the Palace of Westminster for six weeks from 7th August (while Parliament is in recess). Tickets are sent by post. Therefore it is necessary to book four weeks in advance through Ticketmaster – www.ticketmaster.co.uk or contact the Palace of Westminster – Tel: 020-7219-5902. Outside this period it is possible to visit Parliament by arranging it through the New Zealand High Commission which has a small daily allocation of tickets for the Strangers' Gallery at the House of Commons.

Outside the Houses of Parliament on the north side of New Palace Yard is the white stone statue of King George V who, as Duke of Cornwall and York, visited New Zealand with his wife, the future Queen Mary, in 1901.

In order to celebrate the visit to Auckland of the Heir Apparent and his wife Sir John Logan Campbell, the "Father of Auckland", presented some four hundred acres of the huge estate of One Tree Hill to the city of Auckland and requested that it be known as Cornwall Park in honour of the royal guests. This statue of the Queen's grandfather looks out across the road to another distinctive statue which stands in the grounds of the House of Lords but is clearly visible from the street. This is of the regicide, Oliver Cromwell, after whom the town of Cromwell in Otago was named.

A few yards away is Parliament Square which contains several statues of eminent statesmen including Sir Winston Churchill, who once described New Zealand as "the brightest jewel in the British Crown".

Among his many honours and titles Churchill was a gold badge holder of the New Zealand Returned Servicemen's Association, the gold badge having been pinned on his lapel by Lord Freyberg in 1957 on behalf of the R.S.A. He was also awarded the gold badge of the South African War Veterans' Association of New Zealand, a not inappropriate gesture in view of Churchill's daring escape from the Boers. Many of the things that Churchill said were controversial but no one would dispute his statement in 1945 on New Zealand's contribution to the war – "New Zealand never once put a foot wrong".

There is also a statue of Lord Palmerston, the Victorian Prime Minister of Great Britain after whom the city of Palmerston North and the town of Palmerston in Otago are named. On one occasion, when a General Election was coming up, Lord Palmerston, already well into his seventies, was the leader of the Liberal Party while his Conservative opponent was Disraeli. During the campaign it came to the attention of the Conservatives that the wily old Palmerston had a mistress who was barely eighteen. They went to Disraeli and asked if they should reveal the scandal to the voters. "Good God, no," he replied, "if that became known he would sweep the country."

Lord Palmerston lived at No.94 Piccadilly which was later the Naval and Military Club, known as the "In and Out" because of its two gates – one for entrance, the other for exit. From here Palmerston used to walk down to Parliament and his journey took him past the famous Carlton Club, whose members were the opposition Conservatives. The Carlton Club was one of the first buildings to get a flushing toilet and each morning Lord Palmerston, the Liberal Prime Minister, would drop in to use it even though he was not a member of the club. The other members were somewhat reluctant to confront the Prime Minister over such a sensitive matter so – brave men that they were - they told the club's doorman to approach the great Palmerston on his next visit. The following morning the Prime Minister dropped in for his usual call and the doorman asked him if he was a member. "Good God," exclaimed Palmerston, "is this place a club as well?" So Palmerston North and Palmerston, Otago, were named after quite a character!

From Parliament Square one can see the high Gothic towers of Westminster Abbey, the church where the Sovereign is crowned in a ceremony that goes back to Saxon times. The Unknown Warrior is buried under the floor of the Abbey, the body of this unknown soldier having been brought from the Western Front and buried here with great formality on 12th November, 1920.

The Unknown Warrior belongs to New Zealand as much as to Britain since the Anzacs were fighting alongside their British cousins in that sector of the Western Front where he fell. In his youth he might well have heard the call of the bellbird as he sat under a punga tree with his lady love.

At the burial ceremony of this nameless soldier Lt. Col. Bernard Freyberg V.C., the future General and Governor-General, was in command of the Guard of

Honour which consisted of a hundred Victoria Cross winners. After assembling on the square at nearby Chelsea Barracks and with Freyberg at their head, these brave and noble men marched to Westminster Abbey where they formed two rows on either side of the entrance to the grave. No king or warrior in history has ever had such a Guard of Honour – one hundred of the bravest of the brave.

Buried under the central aisle of the nave of this great church are the ashes of Lord Rutherford, the New Zealand born physicist who split the atom. The memorial of this great scientist, whose portrait is on the New Zealand hundred dollar note, can be seen in the north aisle.

At the end of the aisle is the spot where the Queen was crowned on 2nd June, 1953, in the presence of 7,500 people including the Prime Minister of New Zealand, Sidney Holland. The first Coronation that was held here was that of William the Conqueror on Christmas Day, 1066.

Her Majesty sat on the Coronation Chair. This is also known as Saint Edward's Chair since it was made for Edward I in the thirteenth century and has been used in the coronation of all his successors except Edward V and Edward VIII (who abdicated before he was crowned). Made of oak, it rests on four feet that represent lions – the ancient symbol of monarchy. It can be seen in the Confessor's Chapel. It was on this historic seat that the Queen was crowned by the Archbishop of Canterbury. After the Coronation oath was administered Her Majesty promised to govern according to their respective laws the peoples of "the United Kingdom of Great Britain and Northern Ireland, Canada, Australia, New Zealand, the Union of South Africa, Pakistan and Ceylon, and of her possessions and the other territories to any of them belonging or pertaining" – an oath that she has always carried out with honour, dignity and an unswerving sense of duty.

Beneath the North Transept rose is a set of stained glass windows depicting the Six Acts of Mercy. These are the work of British artist, Brian Thomas, who also designed the six great windows in the nave of Saint Paul's Cathedral in Wellington. Also in the North Transept (in the western aisle) is a tablet in honour of Warren Hastings, the Governor-General of India after whom the Hawkes Bay city of Hastings is named. It was erected by his widow and is situated behind a large tomb. (See: Daylesford, Gloucs)

In the Chapel of the Holy Cross is a tablet that commemorates the million plus servicemen of the British Empire who gave their lives in the First World War. The design of the tablet was the result of consultations with the governments of the Empire – Canada, Australia, New Zealand, South Africa and India. After the Second World War the words were amended to "the wars of 1914 and 1939". It was unveiled in December, 1926, by the Prince of Wales (later King Edward VIII) in the presence of the dominion Prime Ministers – including Gordon Coates of New Zealand - who were in London for an Imperial premiers' conference. Led by the Dean of Westminster, the Prime Ministers formed a procession into the Abbey while the choir and 1,200 congregation sang *Land of Hope and Glory*. "Time can not dim our remembrance of them," said the Prince of Wales.

The actual unveiling took place in the main part of the Abbey, not far from the Tomb of the Unknown Warrior, and the tablet was later moved here to the Chapel of the Holy Cross which itself is a memorial to the war dead of New Zealand and the other parts of the Empire. A truly sacred place to say a prayer.

In the South Cloister of the Abbey is a memorial to three navigators, Drake, Captain Cook and Francis Chichester, the last mentioned of whom made the first solo flight across the Tasman from New Zealand to Australia in Gipsy Moth I, a seaplane. In 1966-7 he made a solo circumnavigation of the world in Gipsy Moth IV, stopping only at Sydney.

Each year on Anzac Day a commemorative service is held in the Abbey following the laying of wreaths at the Cenotaph in Whitehall. Tickets for the ceremony can be obtained from the New Zealand High Commission, 80 Haymarket, London SW1Y 4TQ.

PARKS AND PALACES

"...the great crowds and the beauty and the stateliness of London".

- Richard John Seddon, Prime Minister of New Zealand 1893-1906.

Across the road from the south-west corner of Trafalgar Square is Admiralty Arch, which is the beginning of the Mall that leads to Buckingham Palace. The best times to be in the Mall are for the Trooping of the Colour in June and the Opening of Parliament in November.

The Trooping takes place on a Saturday in the middle of June; for those who have not managed to get a ticket for the actual ceremony (scarce as hen's teeth) it is still worthwhile to go and stand in the Mall and watch the soldiers, horses, massed bands and Royal Family go by. The Duke of Edinburgh and Prince of Wales are usually on horseback in their regimental uniforms, complete with busbees, but the Queen travels in one of her coaches. All the pageantry of old and the magic of monarchy are on display, providing a colourful and magnificent contrast to our increasingly grey and technological world.

In November the Queen and other members of the Royal Family travel along the Mall in horse drawn carriages for the Opening of Parliament at Westminster. This is also a grand occasion, the wide sweep of the tree-lined Mall providing an elegant setting for all the Queen's horses and all the Queen's men.

A few yards along the Mall on the left is a statue of Captain Cook. "He laid the foundation of the British Empire in Australia and New Zealand" reads the inscription. On New Zealand Day in February a wreath is laid at the foot of the statue. The ceremony is arranged by the New Britain Movement which, despite its name, is dedicated to retaining the traditional links between Britain and the dominions.

A short distance past the Captain Cook statue and on the other side of the road are the wide steps leading up to the Duke of York's Column.

Turn left (west) at the base of the Column into Carlton House Terrace with its graceful Regency architecture and a few yards along on the left is No. 6, the home of the Royal Society. This is the oldest and foremost scientific body in the world. Inside its entrance hall is a bust of George III, which was crafted by Joseph Nollekens, a noted sculptor who specialised in nude female figures – his famous Venuses. This bust of George III has an interesting connection with the discovery of New Zealand.

One of the purposes of Captain Cook's first voyage to the Pacific on the *Endeavour* was to take observers to the South Seas to study astronomy and botany in these unknown parts. The Royal Society was therefore a sponsor of Cook's expedition and King George III gave it the sum of £4,000 to cover costs.

The expenses turned out to be less than what had been given and so the Royal Society used the surplus to commission Nollekens to make a bust of the man who was both its King and its benefactor. Thus the bust was paid for with the same donation that financed the discovery of New Zealand.

At the end of the Mall is Buckingham Palace, the home of the Sovereign, the heart of the Commonwealth and the visible symbol of our enduring constitutional monarchy. The flying of the Royal Standard from the flagpole on top of the Palace signifies that the Queen is in residence.

To the right of Buckingham Palace is Constitutional Hill which leads to Hyde Park Corner. This open space is dominated by the great monument to the Duke of Wellington – an arch that Queen Victoria refused to drive under as she did not think that a Sovereign should have to ride under an arch that was dedicated to one of her subjects – not even one as great as the victor of Waterloo.

On the Hyde Park side is Apsley House, a brown sandstone structure, which was the home of the Duke of Wellington and should be of interest to people from New Zealand's capital city. It is open to the public.

When the first settlers moved from Petone to what is now the city of Wellington in September, 1840, they named the new site "Wellington" in honour of the Iron Duke. They were acting on instructions from the New Zealand Company's directors in London who chose the name out of gratitude for the help that the Duke had given to their previous colonising effort in South Australia. An interesting coincidence was that the carved figurehead on the bow of the *Tory*, the ship which brought the first settlers to Wellington, was of the Duke.

Some of the streets of the capital were named after his battles. Salamanca Road and Talavera Terrace, stops on the Kelburn Cable Car route, were named after two of his victories in the Peninsula War in Spain while Waterloo Quay on Wellington's waterfront commemorates his greatest victory as does Waterloo Quadrant in Auckland and the suburb of Waterloo in the Hutt Valley.

Like the city that bears his name, Wellington was a man of contrasts. Plain spoken yet deeply conservative, he was the greatest military commander of the day and yet he was probably the worst shot in the British Isles. During a pheasant shoot at a country house some years after Waterloo a servant girl had her head out the window to watch the action. The Duke took aim at a bird – and shot the servant girl in the head. She tumbled backwards, confused but not dead. Her mistress saw what had happened and exclaimed, "But you are so privileged! You have just been shot by the great Duke of Wellington."

The Duke of Wellington was and still is one of the truly great men of history; New Zealand and the United States are the only two countries in the world to have their capital cities named after major historical figures of sound reputation, both of whom were statesmen as well as soldiers.

The victor of Waterloo lived here at Apsley House for thirty-four years. It is now the Wellington

Museum although the present Duke continues to occupy several rooms in the house as his London residence. The address of this house is simply "Number One, London", the reason being that in former times this was the first house that one reached when riding through the countryside into London from the west.

In the Museum can be seen items of plate and porcelain that were presented to him by the grateful sovereigns of Europe as well as by commercial companies since his victory at Waterloo ended the Napoleonic wars and the economic blockades that were part and parcel of the struggle. Also on display are his decorations, field-marshal's baton and the dressing case that he used on his campaigns which contains a cake of soap two hundred years old, his pills and even his toothbrush!

On the first floor of the building is the ninety foot long Waterloo Gallery where, on each anniversary of the battle until his death in 1852, the Duke gave a dinner for his old officers who all attended in full dress uniform.

Prime Minister from 1828 to 1830, Wellington opposed the passing of the Reform Bill in 1832. This made him unpopular with the advocates of reform and on two occasions the windows of Apsley House were broken by stone throwing mobs which, to put it mildly, showed a certain amount of ingratitude towards the man who saved Europe from the curse of Napoleon.

Behind Apsley House is Hyde Park which, together with the Regent's Park, provides London with its two "open air lungs". After entering Hyde Park from behind Apsley House, follow the Serpentine Road a short distance and you will see on the right - set back slightly from the path - the Cavalry Memorial with a statue of Saint George holding up his sword and the dragon lying dead at his feet.

This memorial was erected by the Cavalry of the Empire for their comrades who lost their lives in two world wars. On the wall of the monument is a list of cavalry regiments of the First World War and on the right are the names of the New Zealand units – the Auckland Mounted Rifles, the Wellington Mounted Rifles, the Canterbury Mounted Rifles and the Otago Mounted Rifles.

These four regiments consisted of some of the best riders in New Zealand. All of them served at Gallipoli as part of the Anzac division. After evacuation from the Dardanelles the Otago Mounted Rifles reformed in Egypt and proceeded to the Western Front where they took so many casualties that they were eventually reduced to a single squadron. The other three mounted regiments took a leading part in the Sinai and Palestine campaigns.

At the north-east corner of Hyde Park, near Marble Arch, is Speakers' Corner which is usually cited as the true test of English liberty where any communist, atheist, fascist or feminist can get up and say what they like. The best time to attend this free entertainment is a Sunday afternoon.

It was at Speakers' Corner that Peter Fraser, the wartime Prime Minister of New Zealand, made his first public speech and honed his skills as a debater. So, if you hear someone carrying on like a fanatic, don't write him off as an oddball; he might well finish up as the Prime Minister of New Zealand!

To the west of Hyde Park is Kensington Gardens which surround Kensington Palace. This graceful building was the home of the late Diana, Princess of Wales. In front of the palace is a statue of Queen Victoria which was carved by her daughter, Princess Beatrice, an accomplished sculptress. Victoria was born inside Kensington Palace in 1819. The State Apartments are open to the public. Hours: April-October, 9.30 – 5 p.m., November-March, 9.30 – 4 p.m. Inside are furniture and paintings from the Royal Collection. The walls of the Cupola Room are adorned with gilded statues of Roman gods and busts of Roman emperors. This was where Queen Victoria was christened shortly after her birth. The royal font used for the ceremony is on display at the Tower of London as part of the Royal Regalia.

On the western side of the boating lake known as the Long Water is a famous statue of Peter Pan. Visitors from Wanganui should find it familiar since an exact replica of it stands in the park that surrounds Virginia Lake in Wanganui.

To the south of the Long Water is the elaborate Albert Memorial which is dedicated to Prince Albert, the husband of Queen Victoria, after whom the Auckland suburb of Mount Albert was named as well as Auckland's Albert Park.

The Albert Memorial is the epitome of high Victorian architecture. With its medley of marble, granite, mosaic and bronze and the ornate canopy over the ten ton statue of the Prince Consort, it is a welcome relief from the austerity and dullness that characterise so much of modern architecture – especially memorials. The frieze surrounding the base includes about 170 life size figures carved in relief.

The site was chosen because of its proximity to the Crystal Palace that housed the Great Exhibition of 1851. The great glass structure, that many people thought would be shattered in the first hail storm, was situated in the Park near Rutland Gate. This international exposition of British products was the first of its kind and was the brainchild of Prince Albert. His other claims to fame were that he introduced Christmas trees to Britain (and thereby to New Zealand) and he was instrumental in preventing war between Great Britain and the northern states during the American Civil War when he rose from his death-bed and toned down a particularly hostile telegram that Lord Palmerston, the Prime Minister, was sending to President Lincoln.

The profits of the Great Exhibition were so huge that they financed the building of all the nearby museums of South Kensington – the Victoria and Albert, the Science Museum and the Museum of Natural History as well as the Imperial College of Science and the Royal Albert Hall. They also provided scholarships to Oxford and Cambridge which are still in existence to-day. It is interesting to compare the success of the Great Exhibition with the Dome that the British Government built at Greenwich to celebrate the

Millennium. Ugly in both design and contents, this great financial flop cost the British taxpayer more than £800,000,000. Progress since 1851?

Prince Albert looks out across the road known as Kensington Gore to the Royal Albert Hall behind which are several colleges and museums, including the Museum of Natural History which fronts on to Cromwell Road. Among its many treasures is Sir Joseph Banks' botany collection which includes several specimens that he collected in New Zealand when he arrived with Captain Cook.

The road to the west of the Natural History Museum is Queen's Gate, which leads back to Kensington Gardens. Four blocks west is a quiet street known as De Vere Gardens. The houses here are known as "mews" and were originally the stables for nearby Kensington Palace. It was in a four storeyed house in this street that Kiri Te Kanawa and her husband, Desmond Park, lived for two years after their marriage in 1967.

A few blocks further along on the other side of Kensington High Street can be seen all the flags in front of the Commonwealth Institute. On the side wall of the large brick building alongside this mass of flagpoles is a blue plaque stating that it was the home of Sir David Low, the Dunedin born cartoonist who achieved fame in the 1930s for his cartoons in the London Evening Standard which ridiculed Hitler – among others. There is a blue plaque outside No. 33 to record Low's residence here.

WEST LONDON

"So sits enthroned in vegetable pride
Imperial Kew by Thames's glittering side."

- Thomas Chatterton on Kew Gardens, 1770

Southfields station is on the green District Line to Wimbledon. This is where one gets off to go to the Wimbledon tennis championships which take place in the last week of June and the first week of July each year. However, if one visits Wimbledon on one of the other fifty weeks of the year there is still the tennis museum to see as well as a large reference library. These are open every day of the year from 10.30 a.m. to 5 p.m. However, during the fortnight of the Championships the museum and library are open only to those who have tickets for the tennis.

The museum is arranged in chronological order. The name of Christchurch born Anthony Wilding can be seen on the Edwardians' Panel.

The "Way to Wimbledon" from Southfields station is along Wimbledon Park Road and into Church Road and the All England Lawn Tennis and Croquet Club is on the right. Many New Zealanders associate Wimbledon with Anthony Wilding, who won the Men's Singles Championship four times (1910, 1911, 1912 and 1913), the only New Zealander ever to have done so. However, Wilding did not play at the present Wimbledon venue for in his day the Championships were played at the old site in Worple Road,

Wimbledon, where there was more of a garden party atmosphere. The All England Club moved to the present site in 1922. However, the Centre Court at modern Wimbledon has resounded to the thud of New Zealand feet. Onny Parun played on its sacred turf in 1972 and 1979 while in 1983 Chris Lewis played in the Final against John McEnroe, a contest that the American won.

From 1966 to 1981 the All England Club leased twelve acres of its land to the London New Zealand Rugby Football Club and they named their ground Aorangi Park which means "Cloud in the Sky". The club had 700 members, five rugby teams and tennis and cricket clubs. There were two rugby fields, eighteen tennis courts, a cricket pitch and a bowling green. The lease ended in 1981 and the All England Club took back the land for its tennis facilities. However, the Aorangi name can still be seen at Wimbledon during the Championships in the Aorangi Picnic Terrace, Aorangi Food Court and Aorangi Café.

Take a District Line train back from Southfields and change at Earl's Court to a Richmond train. This will stop at Kew, the site of the famous Kew Gardens, which cover some three hundred acres. Plants have been brought to Kew from the four corners of the world, including rubber plants from Brazil which were raised here and then sent to Malaya to start its huge rubber industry.

The first New Zealand plants to arrive at Kew were those which Sir Joseph Banks brought back on the *Endeavour* when he accompanied Captain Cook on his first voyage to the Pacific in 1768-70. The furthering of botanical knowledge was one of the purposes of Cook's journey and there were two botanists on board (Banks and Daniel Solander, a Swede) and they had eight assistants, including two artists to draw the plants.

When the *Endeavour* pulled into Tolaga Bay on the East Coast Banks and his team collected and dried more than a hundred and sixty plants and at Mercury Bay on the Coromandel Peninsula they took another two hundred. When the *Endeavour* and its crew rested at Ship Cove in the Queen Charlotte Sound, its keen botanists collected another two hundred plants as this was the only place in the South Island where they landed and, of course, the South Island had many plants that were not to be found in the north.

Banks had a passion for botany and elected to study natural history at Oxford rather than the usual Classics. He was the gardener and unofficial director at Kew from 1772 to 1819 during which time he added about 7,000 exotic plants to the Kew collection, thereby establishing its world wide reputation. He also sent botanical collections to other countries – including New Zealand. Just inside the Main Gate to the right is the Sir Joseph Banks Building which is named in his honour. Banks died on 19th June, 1820. By his express wish, this rich and famous man, friend of both George III and Captain Cook, was buried in a simple grave at Saint Leonard's church at Heston, West London.

However, even more New Zealand flora was sent to Kew by Sir Joseph Hooker who arrived in New Zealand in 1841 at the age of twenty-five. A keen botanist with a flair for drawing, he sketched many of the plants that he sent back to Kew where his father was the Director. When he returned to England he wrote an illustrated book on the plant life of New Zealand which was published in 1864.

Hooker succeeded his father as Director at Kew and continued to receive New Zealand plants from such keen botanists as William Colenso and Sir Julius von Haast. In turn forest plants were sent from Kew to help the New Zealand timber industry. The scientific study of a new country's plant life is necessary for its development and much of the study of New Zealand plants was done here at Kew.

In Kew's Museum of Plants and People can be seen a woven bag made from New Zealand flax (phormium tenax). This is displayed in the glass case entitled "The Collections' Origins" while in Showcase No. 3 ("Fabulous Fabrics"), on the left of the entrance foyer, are some fibre and Scotch twilled sheeting made from New Zealand flax.

Another of Kew's buildings of interest to New Zealanders is the Marianne North Art Gallery. This artist visited New Zealand in 1880 and painted many of our plants and scenes. Her New Zealand paintings are hanging on the right of the gallery entrance and include two of the Otira Gorge (Nos. 714 and 731), a view of Lake Wakatipu (713), Mount Earnslaw from the island in the middle of Lake Wakatipu (723), Castle Hill Station (717) and a group of nikau palms (722). Outside the gallery Australian and New Zealand trees are being planted.

Continuing on the District Line in a westerly direction one comes to Richmond which was formerly a village but is now a busy outer suburb of London. It was here that one of New Zealand's bravest sons was born. From the station turn right and then right again into Church Road. After crossing the intersction with Sheen Road, the first turning on the right is a little street called Dynevor Road and it was here in the three storeyed house at No. 8 that New Zealand's most distinguished soldier, Bernard Freyberg, was born on 21st March, 1889.

Following Church Road up the hill and turning into Friars Style Road and then left into the street known as Richmond Hill, one comes to Richmond Gate at the top. This is the entrance to Richmond Park, described by D.H.Lawrence as "one of the few remaining parts of the old world of romance".

Two thousand, four hundred acres in extent, Richmond is the largest park in London and is a wonderful place at week-ends for running, cycling, showing off or just having a quiet smoke with your friends. Formerly a royal hunting ground, it was enclosed by Charles I in 1637 and is still the home of several hundred deer that roam freely.

Entering the park from Richmond Gate and bearing right, one comes to the park's highest point which is known as King Henry's Mound. From here on a clear day it is possible to see several London landmarks to the east and Windsor Castle to the west. Legend has it that Henry VIII stood here so that he could see the signal indicating that his second wife, the unfortunate Anne Boleyn, had been executed at the Tower of London. At least nobody could ever accuse Henry VIII of being a gentleman!

The town of Richmond near Nelson was named after this attractive borough on the banks of the Thames.

No exploration of West London would be complete without a visit to Twickenham, south-west of Richmond, which is the home of English rugby. This has been the venue of many memorable clashes between the All Blacks and either England or the Barbarians.

The rugby ground of Twickenham dates from 1909. Before that internationals were played at the Oval cricket ground.

Twickenham is part of New Zealand's sporting history and was the venue of what many regard as the most exciting rugby match of all time, the All Blacks v Barbarians match on 16th December, 1967, which the New Zealanders won in the last minute with an unforgettable try by left wing Tony Steel.

It was at Twickenham where the All Black, Cyril Brownlie, was sent off the field by the referee during the tour of the Invincibles in 1924-5. The Prince of Wales (later King Edward VIII) was sitting in the Royal Box and sent a message to the referee asking him to reconsider his decision but it was to no avail. However, retribution was exacted later in the match when the other Brownlie brother, Maurice, scored a try and the All Blacks won.

An even more emotional moment for New Zealanders at this ground was a match at the end of the First World War between the New Zealand Army and the British Army. Although not a Test match it was still a sell-out and among those who attended was the Prime Minister of New Zealand, Bill Massey, who was in Europe for the Peace Conference at Versailles.

As he arrived outside the gates of Twickenham Massey was recognised by several busloads of young New Zealanders who had just disembarked from their coaches. They called out three cheers for their Prime Minister. As Massey walked over to thank them he could see that they were all war amputees with missing limbs. These young men, all in the prime of life, were waving their wooden arms and crutches in the air by way of greeting. It was all too much for Massey; he broke down and cried.

The Museum of Rugby at Twickenham is the largest of its kind in the world and is a "must" for any serious rugby fan. After entering through an original Twickenham turnstile there are many things to see - including a ball that is older than the game of rugby itself, relics of the first British tour abroad (to Australia and New Zealand in 1888), the earliest known rugby film footage, some stately old baths in which players of the 1930s used to loll after a match, old programmes and even a scrum machine on which you can test your strength (not recommended for those over eighty!).

Also on display is the Calcutta Cup which is at stake every time England plays Scotland. It is made from 270 melted down silver rupees donated by the now disbanded Calcutta Football Club in India.

In 1877 the Calcutta Club could not field enough players because so many of its members – soldiers and administrators – had been posted to other places in India or had gone Home. In the true spirit of selfless sportsmanship the club wanted to do some lasting good for the beloved game and so they arranged for a cup to be made out of the silver rupees that were left in the bank account on the sad day when the club closed its doors. A beautiful piece of Indian craftsmanship, it has three handles in the shape of cobras and an elephant on top of the lid.

The Museum, situated at 180 Whitton Road, Twickenham, is open Tuesday-Saturday, 10 a.m.-5 p.m., Sundays 2-5 p.m. and Bank Holidays 10 a.m.-5 p.m. Closed on post matchday Sundays and Mondays, Good Friday, Christmas Eve, Christmas Day and Boxing Day.

One can go on a conducted tour of the stadium at Twickenham (Tel: 020-8892-8877) These take place Tuesday-Saturday and Bank Holidays at 10.30 a.m., 12 noon, 1.30 p.m. and 3 p.m. On Sundays there is one tour at 3 p.m.

The Twickenham Rugby Store (Mail Order Hotline: 020-8891-4141 or www.rfu.com) sells all sorts of jerseys, caps, boots, headgear, scarves, ties, cufflinks, key rings, badges, books and other souvenirs.

The closest station is Twickenham (mainline from Waterloo). Outside the station turn into Whitton

Road and then cross the busy Chertsey Road (A316) into Rugby Road, the home of rugby football.

NORTH LONDON

The area north of the Marylebone Road is blessed with two extensive areas of greenery – the carefully manicured lawns and gardens of the Regent's Park and the more rustic grounds of Hampstead Heath.

On the west side of the Regent's Park (named after the Prince Regent, who became George IV) is Lords Cricket Ground (closest station: Saint John's Wood). Not only is this the main venue for Tests between England and New Zealand but it is the spiritual home of New Zealand's favourite summer sport.

On days that are not Match Days or Preparation Days there are public tours of Lords which include the Long Room, the "Holy of Holies" from which members of the M.C.C. watch the play. The walls of the Long Room are decorated with many fine paintings of cricketers and cricket subjects; there is one of Bradman and another of his nemesis, Douglas Jardine.

The tour also includes the M.C.C. Museum, which is dedicated to all cricketers who died in the two world wars. It is a veritable treasure trove of the game of cricket and its exhibits cover all aspects of the game in various parts of the world. On view are bats that were wielded by the legendary W.G.Grace, Bradman's boots (such small feet for such a great batsman!), and the tiny terracotta urn containing the famous "ashes" which have been contested by Australia and England ever since they were presented by a group of Australian women to the England captain, the Honourable Ivo Bligh, during the M.C.C.'s tour of Australia in 1882-3. There are also several fine paintings of cricket grounds in both the Museum and the Long Room, including one of Auckland's Eden Park by Peter McIntyre. A good time to visit the Museum is during the lunch break at a Test match.

Other features of this "cathedral of cricket" that can be seen on the guided tour are the famous Mound Stand, the practice wickets at the Nursery End, the tennis court (real tennis) and the Lords Shop where one can buy prints, books, ties and cricket equipment. Shop opening times: Monday-Friday, 10 a.m.- 5.p.m.; Weekends, 11 a.m.- 4 p.m.

To book a Lords tour, telephone 7432-1033. The times are noon and 2 p.m. throughout the year and an extra tour at 10 a.m. from April to September. One can round off the tour with a drink or three at the Lords Tavern, which is just outside the Grace Gates.

The M.C.C. Library at Lords contains the most comprehensive collection of cricket books and manuscripts in the world. Cricket writers and others may use it by contacting the Curator on (020) 7289-1611.

A mile north of the Regent's Park is Hampstead Heath (closest Tube: Hampstead on the Northern Line – Edgeware branch) The area around Hampstead Heath is one of the more desirable residential parts of London and it was here that Katherine Mansfield (1888-1923) lived with her husband, John Middleton Murry (1889-

1957). Their home was No. 2 Portland Villas, a white three storeyed house at 17 East Heath Road, right on the edge of the Heath and only a short distance down East Heath Road from Heath Street. There is a blue plaque on the wall of the house recording her residence here. She and her husband called it "the Elephant" and the household included two maids and a drunken cook.

Hampstead has been the home of many writers; indeed there is a saying that everybody in Hampstead has either just finished a novel or is about to start one. Katherine Mansfield married John Middleton Murry in 1918, at the end of the war in which her younger brother, Leslie, was killed. They were close friends (for a time) of D.H.Lawrence, author of *Lady Chatterley's Lover* and *Sons and Lovers*, and his wife and the two couples often went for walks together on Hampstead Heath. It is interesting to note that Hampstead Heath is not a park; it is as it always has been - open countryside. However, not even all the walks in the fresh air of the Heath could help poor Katherine Mansfield who contracted tuberculosis and died at the age of thirty-five.

Walking on to Hampstead Heath from East Heath Road and crossing over the bathing ponds, one comes to a rise called Parliament Hill, from which on a clear day one can see the Houses of Parliament. This high point in North London has an interesting connection with one of New Zealand's most cherished traditions – Guy Fawkes Day.

When he had completed his preparations for blowing up Parliament on that famous Fifth of

November, 1605, Guy Fawkes told all his friends to gather on Parliament Hill to watch the blaze. They did but nothing happened. With such a big mouth it was no wonder that Guy Fawkes was caught before he carried out his dastardly deed. The moral of the story is that, if you are going to blow up Parliament, don't blurt it out to your friends!

Four stops north of Hampstead is Colindale, the station for the R.A.F. Museum at Hendon. Among the many exhibits is a Sunderland flying boat that one can walk through. These used to land on Auckland harbour and Evans Bay, Wellington, as they brought travellers from Australia and the Pacific Islands.

Also in north London and not far from Angel station is the Family Records Office where you can trace your English ancestry. Situated in Myddleton Street, behind Rosebery Avenue, it holds birth, death and marriage certificates from 1837 onwards. Hours: Monday-Saturday, 10 a.m.-5 p.m. (late closing 7 p.m. on Tuesdays and Thursdays). Tel: 8392-5300.

On the other side of Angel station is the busy shopping area of Upper Street. The unusual name of this street has nothing to do with either prices or "uppers". At No. 115 Upper Street (opposite St. Mary's church) is the King's Head. This is a public house in front and a small theatre at the back where some of its plays have gone on to success in the West End.

All prices in the pub are in pounds, shillings and pence which, of course, was the currency of New Zealand until 1967. The cash register is an ornate National Cash Register with a wind-up handle and one can enjoy a pint for a couple of guineas in a traditional atmosphere free of the sterility of metrics and decimals. Strongly recommended both for older folk with a nostalgia for former times and for younger people who can get an idea of what life was like in their parents' day. Closing time on Thursday, Friday and Saturday is 2 a.m.

GREENWICH AND THE THAMES

"The most delightful spot of ground in Great Britain".

- Daniel Defoe on Greenwich

Greenwich is famous throughout the world for its old Royal Observatory from which the world's time is calculated as well as longitude. By virtue of its position on the lower reaches of the Thames it has had a long association with ships and the Navy.

The National Maritime Museum in Romney Road, Greenwich, has a whole room devoted to the exploits of Captain Cook with some of his navigation charts on display as well as some relics of the voyage that he made to Australia and New Zealand on the *Endeavour*. There is a famous portrait of Cook by Nathaniel Dance. Cook was painted shortly before he set out on his last and fatal voyage to the Pacific and Dance depicts him as mature and confident. There is also a portrait of the botanist on the Endeavour, Sir Joseph Banks as well as paintings by William Hodge, who was a draughtsman on the *Resolution*. The museum also has a wonderful collection of more than 2,500 models of old ships – including every type that sailed between Britain and New Zealand – as well as numerous maritime paintings and other exhibits, including the astrolabe that was used by Sir Francis Drake who sailed around the world in the *Golden Hind*.

In the grounds of the museum is a life-size bronze statue of Captain Cook. It was sculpted by British born Anthony Stones who lived in New Zealand from 1952 to 1983. A former Head of Design at TVNZ he is a sculptor in the figurative tradition. This extremely talented man has been responsible for some of New Zealand's finest bronze sculpture in recent years. These include the statues of Captain Cook at Gisborne, of pioneer aviatrix Jean Batten at Auckland Airport, of Abel Tasman on the Nelson waterfront, of Lord Freyberg in Auckland (commissioned by the Royal New Zealand R.S.A.) and of former Prime Minister, Peter Fraser, outside the biggest wooden building in the world near Parliament in Wellington. (See: Gloucester and Derby)

In the river next to Greenwich Pier at the bottom of King William Walk are two ships of historical interest, the tall masted *Cutty Sark* and, in its shadow, the 54 foot ketch, *Gipsy Moth IV*. The *Cutty Sark*, an old clipper, was built for the China tea trade in 1879. Later she took wool from Australia to England.

Gipsy Moth IV is the craft on which Francis Chichester sailed single handed around the world in 1966-7, calling only at Sydney. Upon his return he was knighted by the Queen in the Grand Square of the Royal

Naval College at Greenwich with the same sword that Queen Elizabeth I had used to dub Sir Francis Drake,

Chichester also made the first solo flight across the Tasman sea from New Zealand to Australia in a plane called *Gipsy Moth I*. In fact, altogether he had five Gipsy Moths – four boats and a plane. In his early life Chichester emigrated to New Zealand where, with a business partner, he bought land above Trentham at the top of the Hutt Valley and planted trees on it.

These two boats are open to the public from April to October, Monday – Saturday, 11 – 6 p.m. and Sundays 12 – 6 p.m.

The association between Greenwich and New Zealand goes right back to Captain Cook. The Thames River, which flows into the Hauraki Gulf, was so named by Cook because it seemed to his nautical eye to be as wide as the Thames at Greenwich.

In the New Zealand story Greenwich and, further down the river, Gravesend, and on the other bank, Tilbury, are like liquid history because it was from these points on London's river that so many emigrant ships sailed for New Zealand. A passage from here to New Zealand normally took two to three months – in cramped conditions and with poor hygiene which facilitated the spread of diseases like typhoid. John Lambton, the first Earl of Durham, after whom Wellington's Lambton Quay is named, once said that you could always tell an emigrant ship, even at gunshot range, by its terrible smell.

The first shipload of emigrants to leave Gravesend for New Zealand were those on the *Aurora*, which brought the founding settlers to Wellington. She sailed from here on 22nd September, 1839, reaching Port Nicholson on 22nd January, 1840, and Wellington's anniversary has been celebrated as a public holiday on that day ever since.

It was from Gravesend on 27th April, 1841, that the barques *Whitby* and *Will Watch* left on their way to form the second of the New Zealand Company's settlements at Nelson. Captain Arthur Wakefield, R.N. was in command and on board were a chief surveyor, six assistant surveyors, ten apprentices and seventy-eight labourers. Their task was to explore and find a site for the settlement, peg out the sections and build shelters, tracks and roads. A store ship, the brig *Arrow*, departed three weeks later with the tools and supplies for the new settlement – wagons, survey instruments, small boats for river navigation, forges, tools, tents and pre-fabricated barracks. The *Whitby* and *Will Watch* were pulled down the Thames from Gravesend by steam tugs all the way to Margate where they took off in full sail. All three ships entered Nelson harbour on Guy Fawkes Day, 1841.

The first settlers to arrive in Otago left from Gravesend on 24th November, 1847. There were ninety-six of them on board the *John Wickliffe* and their leader was Captain William Cargill, who was the New Zealand Company's agent for the new settlement. The city of Invercargill is named after him.

Three years later the barque, *Cressy,* which was one of the famous first four ships of the Canterbury settlement, sailed from Gravesend on 4th September, 1850.

Many of the vessels carrying the men of the Royal New Zealand Fencibles and their families sailed from Gravesend around this time, including the *Minerva* and the *Sir Robert Sale* which set sail from here to New Zealand on the same day in 1847. These soldier-settlers and their families formed much of the founding bloodstock of the Auckland settlements of Howick, Otahuhu, Onehunga and Mount Wellington.

Another group of settlers to sail from Gravesend were the colonists for the Non-Conformist settlement that was being established at Albertland on the Kaipara harbour in Northland. The first of these ships, the *Matilda Wattenbach* and the *Hanover*, departed from the East India Dock to the farewell waves of 15,000 people. When they reached Gravesend they stopped for more speeches and farewells. The later ships carrying more of these Non-Conformists to their settlement in North Auckland also sailed from Gravesend. These were the *William Miles*, *Gertrude*, *Tyburnia, Annie Wilson*, and *John Duncan*. However, when they arrived many of the passengers opted to stay in Auckland rather than trek north to Kaipara. In doing so, they provided Auckland with an important element of its pioneer population.

The reason for such a strange name as Gravesend is that it was formerly the custom to throw dead bodies into the Thames. Then a law was passed which imposed an imaginary line across the river at this point. Below the line corpses could still be disposed of but not above it. Hence the name "Gravesend".

KENT

"Kent, Sir, - everybody knows Kent – Apples, cherries, hops and women".

- Charles Dickens, *Pickwick Papers.*

Canterbury

This ancient cathedral city and archepiscopal see gave its name to the largest province in the South Island. Canterbury in New Zealand was settled by the Canterbury Association, which was a Church of England colonising organisation. It was established in 1848 for the purpose of founding an Anglican settlement in distant New Zealand. The then Archbishop of Canterbury, John Sumner, was the head of the organisation and the name of the new province was in honour of both him and the Church of England while the Christchurch suburb of Sumner was in honour of his family name.

The Canterbury settlers were nothing if not ambitious; within only a few years they had dug a railway tunnel under the Port Hills (the Moorhouse Tunnel) and had established both Christ's College and Canterbury College which later became Canterbury University.

When it was decided in the 1960s to build a university here in Canterbury, Kent, they were unable to call it the "University of Canterbury" since that name was already being used in Christchurch, New Zealand, and in the long established custom of academia it is not possible to have the same name for two universities anywhere in the world. Thus it was that the new university had to be called "The University of Kent at Canterbury".

A piece of stone was taken from the wall of Canterbury Cathedral and presented to the new cathedral of Saint Paul's in Wellington by the current Archbishop of Canterbury, Doctor Carey. In Wellington it is embedded into the wall above the "Canterbury door" which opens on to Molesworth Street. Inscribed on this piece of white stone is a cross which is a copy of one that was carved in the eighth century.

Situated in the Crypt of Canterbury Cathedral is the Treasury which contains the crozier and baton of Henry Lascelles Jenner (1820-98) who was consecrated the first Bishop of Dunedin in 1866.

SUSSEX

East Grinstead

> We are McIndoe's army,
> We are his Guinea Pigs.
> With demonstrations and pedicles,
> Glass eyes, false teeth and wigs.
> And when we get our discharge
> We'll shout with all our might:
> *"Per ardua ad astra"*
> We'd rather drink than fight.
>
> - *The Guinea Pig Anthem*

This town in West Sussex on the A22 is best known for its Queen Victoria Hospital, situated in Holtye Road approximately a mile from the centre of town. It was here that the great New Zealand surgeon, Sir Archibald McIndoe, had his plastic surgery clinic which remade the faces of the Air Force pilots who had been burned in their planes in the Battle of Britain and afterwards.

Dunedin born Sir Archibald arrived at the Queen Victoria Hospital within hours of war being declared in 1939 to set up his famous Burns Centre. As the Battle of Britain raged in the skies above he and his skilled team worked long hours to repair the shattered faces and limbs of the young airmen, all in the prime of life.

It was while some of them were recovering in one of the newly erected wooden huts at the hospital that the suggestion was made to form a club of ex-patients; since plastic surgery was in its infancy and a lot of the work was experimental, they decided to call it the Guinea Pig Club. The secretary was a pilot with burned fingers, which excused him from writing letters, while the treasurer was one with burned legs, which meant that he could not run off with the funds.

By the end of the War there were 649 Guinea Pigs, of whom 8% were New Zealanders. Sir Archibald McIndoe was the Club's president from its founding until his death in 1960 when the Duke of Edinburgh took over. The 170 survivors still have a week-end reunion in East Grinstead every year, thereby showing how a full life can be lived in spite of adversity.

To honour the memory of this outstanding New Zealander, whose work in the heat of battle pioneered modern plastic surgery, there are among the buildings of the Queen Victoria Hospital the Blond McIndoe Research Centre, the hospital's McIndoe ward, the McIndoe Surgical Centre and a special garden dedicated to the Guinea Pig Club which was opened in 2000 by Sir Archibald's widow.

On the first floor of the hospital's American wing is a museum which contains photographs and other exhibits, including equipment used by McIndoe and his team. The museum is open to the public on Wednesday afternoons, 2 p.m. - 4 p.m. when the knowledgeable curator is on hand to answer any questions.

Burwash

Along the A265, which leads off the A21 between Tunbridge Wells and Hastings, is the village of Burwash which was the home of Rudyard Kipling (1865-1936) and his wife, Caroline. From 1902 to 1936 they lived at Batemans, a manor house on the edge of the village. It is possible to visit the house and see the rooms exactly as they were when Kipling lived here and penned his poems and stories. His old Rolls Royce is still in the garage.

This famous bard of the British Empire visited New Zealand in 1891, his ship being escorted into Wellington harbour by the famous dolphin, Pelorous Jack, the only individual fish in the world to be protected by an Act of Parliament.

In Christchurch he visited one of his old Latin masters from England, who was a professor at the university, and he regarded all that he saw with such favour that he put some of it into verse. In *Song of the Cities* he wrote of Auckland:

"Last, loneliest, loveliest, exquisite, apart -
On us, on us the unswerving season smiles,
Who wonder mid our fern why men depart
To seek the Happy Isles!"

while in *The Flowers* he alluded to Wellington thus:
"Broom behind the windy town, pollen of the pine –
Bell-bird in the leafy deep where the ratas twine –
Fern above the saddle-bow, flax upon the plain –
Take the flower and turn the hour, and kiss your love again!"

The present gardens at Batemans were created by the Kiplings with Rudyard designing the pond and planting the yew hedge. Indeed, Kipling used some of the money from the Nobel Prize for Literature that he won in 1907 to lay out the gardens. It is nice to think that money that was derived from the Nobel family's dirty business of manufacturing dynamite, which has killed millions of people in wars, was used for a purpose as noble as creating an English country garden.

At the far end of the garden is a small stream, the Dudwell, which features in several of the episodes of his books for children, *Puck of Pook's Hill* and *Rewards and Fairies*. His two young children, Elsie and John, were the originals of Una and Dan in *Puck of Pook's Hill* while the "bare, fern covered slope" of Pook's Hill rises to the west.

It was here at Batemans that the Kiplings suffered a terrible tragedy when their only son, John, was killed in the First World War.

In Kipling's book lined library it is possible to see the ten foot long writing table where he wrote his poems while smoking a pipe "in a blue haze of smoke". The writing table is still in its accustomed place by the window through which the poet could see the trees and fields of Sussex as he penned his verse. On it is a large ink stand which is engraved with the titles of his books.

Although born in India during the British Raj, Kipling loved his adopted county of Sussex of which he wrote:

> God gives all men all earth to love,
> But since our hearts are small
> Ordains for each one spot shall prove
> Beloved over all.
>
> Each to his choice, and I rejoice
> The lot has fallen to me
> In a fair ground – in a fair ground –
> Yea, Sussex by the sea!

Hastings

The city of Hastings in the Hawkes Bay was named after Warren Hastings, the first Governor-General of British India. However, the coincidence of the name with that of the ancient town of Hastings on the Channel coast led to the two towns establishing links with each other although it is not a sister-city relationship. The mayors of Hastings, Sussex, and Hastings, Hawkes Bay, exchange Christmas cards and there have been presentations of gifts. In the Mayor's office of Hastings, New Zealand, is a brass commemorative plaque showing the Battle of Hastings in 1066.

Alfriston

The small village of Alfriston, two miles inland from Seaford, gave its name to the settlement of Alfriston in south Auckland. During the rationing period of the Second World War and immediately afterwards the women of Alfriston, New Zealand, made up food and clothing parcels and sent them to the people of Alfriston, Sussex.

Brighton

"Brighton, that always looks brisk, gay and gaudy, like a harlequin's jacket"

- William Thackeray, *Vanity Fair*, 1847

This large seaside town on the south coast, made famous by the Prince Regent, was the inspiration for the beach resort of New Brighton in Christchurch where they even built an entertainment pier after the fashion of Brighton Pier that juts out into the English Channel. Unlike its Canterbury offspring, Brighton's beach is pebbles and not sand. The beachside settlement of Brighton, south of Dunedin, is also named after the English Brighton.

SURREY

Epsom

South of London on the A24 is the town of Epsom, best known as the site of the Derby which is run in June and is one of the highlights of the London Season. The Auckland suburb of Epsom was named by Lieutenant-Colonel Wynyard after this famous racing town. It was at Epsom in Auckland that the first organised race meeting in New Zealand took place on 5th January, 1842, when some nags ran over some fairly rough ground – a far cry from the carefully prepared track and manicured lawns of the venue of the English Derby.

Walton-on-Thames

This was the site of the No.2 New Zealand General Hospital which, like its counterpart at Brockenhurst in Hampshire, was established to treat those New Zealanders who had been wounded at Gallipoli and on the Western Front and were brought to England in hospital ships. It was staffed by New Zealand nurses and other young women who, although not professional nurses, had paid their own fares from New Zealand and were contributing to the war effort.

The hospital was in a country house known as Mount Felix at Oatlands Park. It was demolished in the 1960s but the stone gate pillars at its entrance can still be seen near the junction of Bridge Street and Oatlands Drive (just before the Walton bridge).

Thousands of wounded Anzacs passed through these gates on their way in and out of the hospital. Following the path around the back of the office building on the right, one reaches the clock tower which is the only remaining part of the building that housed the New Zealand Hospital.

The presence of all these soldiers in Walton-upon-Thames during these difficult years is remembered in the town's New Zealand Avenue and the Wellington pub at 60 High Street, which was named after our capital city and is a "must" for thirsty Wellingtonians in this part of Surrey. There are many pubs in Britain that are named "Wellington" after the conqueror of Napoleon but this is the only one that is named specially after Wellington, New Zealand. It is easily identifiable by its pub sign which shows a map of New Zealand. A good background for a photograph! And for a drink; the pub stocks bottles of Steinlager. During the First World War it was known as the "Kiwi" and its bars resonated to the colonial accents of the recuperating Anzacs who drank their beer and smoked their cigarettes in here as they talked of their dead comrades and planned what they would do when they got back home.

In the churchyard extension of Saint Mary's in Church Street, Walton-on-Thames, are the graves of nineteen New Zealand soldiers who died of their wounds. There is a tall, stone memorial recording their names. Each year on the Sunday closest to Anzac Day there is an evening parade and service at the church which is a continuing link between distant New Zealand and this beautiful town on the Thames which was so familiar to many of our grandfathers and great-grandfathers.

Virginia Water

When the early colonists settled in Wanganui in the nineteenth century they found a charming lake that reminded them of Virginia Water in Surrey and so they named it Virginia Lake. To-day the Wanganui lake is surrounded by the trees and gardens of Virginia Park. Those who have enjoyed a picnic or a walk in its kauri plantation or camellia grove might like to visit Surrey's Virginia Water, two miles east of Walton-on-Thames, and make a comparison.

Virginia Water comprises 160 acres of lake in the south-eastern corner of Windsor Great Park. It was laid out in 1746 by the Duke of Cumberland who, because of his cruelty towards the Scots after the Battle of Culloden, is known to history as "Butcher Cumberland". He was also responsible for getting the sport of boxing banned in England for many years because he lost £10,000 when the fighter he had backed in a match, Jack Broughton, was blinded and lost to a butcher called Jack Slack. Perhaps Cumberland's laying out of beautiful Virginia Water and its environs was an attempt to redeem an otherwise dreadful reputation.

On the south side of the lake is a colonnade of pillars, some broken, which were brought over from Leptis Magna, the ancient city in North Africa, and were re-erected here by George IV who had a good eye for beauty and fine things. One day in 1826 George IV invited his little niece to Windsor Castle and brought her to Virginia Water on an outing. This was the future Queen Victoria, after whom Wanganui's main street, Victoria Avenue, is named.

There are some lovely picnic areas around the lake as well as boating facilities and it is easy to see why this delightful spot inspired the naming of the Wanganui lake.

Brookwood, Woking

Three miles west of Woking on the A324 is Brookwood Military Cemetery. Lying in a beautiful setting of heath, woodland and small hills, this is the resting place of 230 New Zealand servicemen – 148 from the First World War and 82 from the Second. Although the white headstones are identical each is hiding an untold story of the courage and generosity of a young New Zealander who was called upon to make the supreme sacrifice for freedom.

Brookwood is the largest Commonwealth war cemetery and the most heavily populated civilian cemetery in Britain (240,000 graves). To reach the New Zealand section from the main entrance on the Pirbright Road (A324), proceed in a straight line along Saint Lawrence Avenue, then through the American section and past the Stone of Remembrance; the New Zealand graves are the second from the end.

On the first Sunday of every month the Last Post is sounded in the cemetery at sunset.

The cemetery is open every day. Hours: 1st April-30th September, 8 a.m.-7.30 p.m. or dusk, if earlier. From 1st October to 31st March, 8 a.m.-4 p.m. or dusk, if earlier.

Guildford

Guildford Cathedral was the first new cathedral to be consecrated (1961) in the south-east of England since the Reformation. It stands on the summit of Stag

Hill and overlooks the city of Guildford. The land on which it was built was donated by Lord Onslow, the son of the Lord Onslow who was Governor of New Zealand from 1888 to 1892. A memorial tablet on the exterior wall of the Baptistry below the South Window records Lord Onslow's gift.

Guildford is one of the few cathedrals to be built of brick; all the bricks are made of clay which was extracted from the hill on which it stands; thus it rose out of its own green hill! Its design is basic Gothic, the interior being a masterpiece of the controlled use of space, light and shade. One of its features is a Children's Chapel with a particularly small altar. The first thing that one sees upon entering the cathedral at the South Porch is the glass screen of the entrance on which are engraved figures of angels playing the trumpet, the harp and the psaltery (an ancient stringed instrument). The inspiration for this magnificent work of craftsmanship came from the 150th Psalm: "Praise Him with the sound of the trumpet, Praise Him upon the lute and harp." These were etched by John Hutton, a former pupil of Wanganui Collegiate. His work can also be seen in Coventry Cathedral and Saint Paul's Cathedral in Wellington. (See: Coventry)

On the south-eastern edge of Guildford is New Road (A248). A north turn from this thoroughfare into Blacksmith Lane, Chilworth, will bring you into Halfpenny Lane. A short distance up on the right is a car-park with a walking track leading up through the oak trees to the church of Saint Martha-on-the-Hill.

It was within its ancient walls that New Zealand's most distinguished soldier, Bernard Freyberg, was married to Barbara McLaren on 14th June, 1922. J.M.Barrie, the famous playwright who wrote *Peter Pan*, was the Best Man. Then, forty-one years later, after his death at Windsor in 1963, Lord Freyberg was buried here in the churchyard. His coffin, draped with the Union Jack, was carried up the path to Saint Martha's. Freyberg's grave is just outside the south door of the church.

Clandon

To the east of Guildford on the A25 is the village of West Clandon with its splendid country mansion, Clandon Park, which has been the home of the Onslow family since 1641. The house is a combination of Palladian, Baroque and European style while the grounds were laid out by the most famous landscape gardener of all time, Capability Brown. Clandon Park was the home of the Earl of Onslow who became Governor of New Zealand in 1888 at the age of thirty-five, the youngest man ever to hold the office. He was the first of three earls to be appointed Governor, the office previously being held by mere knights!

When Lord Onslow's second son was born at Government House, Wellington, in 1890 he was the first vice-regal baby ever to be born in New Zealand. It was felt to be all the more auspicious since 1890 was the year that New Zealand was celebrating the 50th Anniversary of its founding on the lawn at Waitangi.

The Onslow baby was named Victor Alexander Herbert Huia, the last being the name of the native bird that symbolised nobility. Throughout his life he was always called "Huia".

So excited were the people of New Zealand at this apparently auspicious birth that they sent a petition to Queen Victoria asking her to be the godmother. She graciously acceded to their request and at the christening of the infant at Old Saint Paul's in Wellington on 26th January, 1891, his mother, the Countess of Onslow, stood in for the Great White Queen across the sea. The Mayor of Welllington, Mr. C.J.Johnston, was the godfather "to represent all the people of New Zealand".

The Maoris made the baby boy a chieftain of the Ngatahuia tribe and the chieftain's cloak of kiwi feathers that was presented to the infant is on display in the Blue Wallpaper Room of Clandon House. In the same room can be seen a display cabinet of New Zealand greenstone.

Unfortunately this advantageous start in life for Huia Onslow did not lead to happiness for, when he was twenty, he dived into a lake in the Dolomites in Italy and struck his head on a submerged rock, injuring his spinal cord. For the remaining eleven years of his life he was a paralysed wreck, finally dying at the age of thirty-one.

The Earl of Onslow's last act as Governor was to sign a law giving statutory protection to the fast disappearing native bird after whom his son was named.

The Wellington suburb of Onslow commemorates this interesting family.

In the grounds of Clandon Park is a genuine eighteenth century Maori meeting house which the earl shipped home while he was Governor. When it was purchased by Lord Onslow it had been standing derelict for three years, having been the only building in its area to survive the eruption of Mount Tarawera on 10th June, 1886. It stood at the entrance to Te Wairoa, better known as "The Buried Village" near Rotorua. It had been used by local Maoris to entertain tourists who came to view the spectacular Pink and White Terraces. When the mountain blew its top people ran into the meeting house for shelter, its steep roof allowing the mud to slide off. Inside the building the frightened occupants used wooden benches to prop up the sagging roof.

As his governorship drew to a close the Earl of Onslow wanted to take a piece of New Zealand back to Clandon as a memento and what could be better than the meeting house with such an interesting history? He bought it for £50 (the original Bill of Sale can be seen inside Clandon House) and shipped it home where it has graced the grounds of Clandon Park ever since. There is also a parterre and grotto while the inside of the house is famous for its two storey marble hall and fine Italian plaster work that depicts scenes from mythology.

Clandon Park is owned by the National Trust and is open from the beginning of April until the end of

October on Tuesday, Wednesday, Thursday and Sunday, 11 a.m. – 5 p.m.

BERKSHIRE

Crowthorne

At Crowthorne in Berkshire, two miles north of Camberley, are the impressive buildings of Wellington College – "the monument to the memory of the dear old Duke", wrote Queen Victoria in her diary on 3rd June, 1856, when she laid the foundation stone. Wellington College in Berkshire is a public school where many of the pupils are, appropriately for a school named after the victor of Waterloo, the sons of army officers. In England the term "public school" is the equivalent of a private school in New Zealand. As a rather exclusive fee-paying school Wellington College in Berkshire is quite different from its namesake in New Zealand which started as a grammar school and is now a state school. During the Second World War and the rationing period that followed the boys of Wellington College, New Zealand, sent food parcels to the pupils of Wellington College, Berkshire, to supplement the meagre wartime and post-war diet.

Windsor and Eton

"Ye distant spires, ye antique towers,
That crown the wat'ry glade..."

- Thomas Gray, *Ode on a Distant Prospect of Eton College*

Although Eton is technically within the county of Buckinghamshire we shall deal with it here since it is close to Windsor and one does not normally visit the one without visiting the other.

The town of Eton is dominated by the tall tower of its famous school which, like Wellington College, has several interesting links with New Zealand. Eton is not the oldest "public school" (private school by New Zealand standards) in England; that honour rests with Winchester which was founded 46 years earlier.

Eton was founded in 1440 by Henry VI who, at the age of nineteen, was not much more than a schoolboy himself. Its school buildings straddle both sides of the High Street and the most prominent building is the Chapel which stands above the Thames. On the wall of the ante-chapel is a bronze tablet in memory of a former chaplain, Henry John Chitty Harper, who was the first bishop of Christchurch in New Zealand. Part of the Latin inscription translates as "....his aim was to govern others by becoming the servant of all". Also in the chapel is a memorial to Bishop Abraham, the first bishop of Wellington.

Several of New Zealand's Governors-General have been educated at Eton including Sir Charles Fergusson, Sir Bernard Fergusson, Lord Bledisloe and Lord Cobham as well as the Duke of Wellington and Sir Joseph Banks. The Provost (headmaster) of Eton from 1994 to 2002 was Auckland born Mr. John Lewis. Committed to the Christian ethos of the school, Mr. Lewis oversaw the education of both our future king, Prince William, and his younger brother, Prince Harry. Another recent link with New Zealand is that Mr. Ian McKinnon, the headmaster of Scots College, Wellington from 1992 to 2002 and the brother of former Foreign Minister Don McKinnon, was Lower Master (Deputy Headmaster) at Eton from 1988 to 1992.

Between the end of March and the beginning of October there are daily tours of Eton at 2.15 and 3.15 p.m. (Assemble at the main office of the school entrance) During the rest of the year the Chapel is usually open in the afternoons (2 - 4.30 p.m.) during Term and in the mornings during the holidays.

Windsor is dominated by its royal castle. Founded by William the Conqueror, it is the largest inhabited castle in the world. It is now fully restored after the terrible fire of 1992 which damaged more than a hundred rooms. The Queen and members of her family spend most week-ends here and it is from within its walls that she makes her Christmas broadcast to the people of the Commonwealth although in 1953 she made it from Auckland.

It is possible to visit the State Apartments and view their historic treasures. They are open all year round except for a few occasions when there is a State visit or private function. To check, telephone (01753) 869-898.

The most important event at Windsor each year is the Garter ceremony which takes place on the Monday closest to 18th June. The Queen leads the members of England's oldest order of knighthood in their colourful robes from the State Apartments down the hill to Saint George's Chapel where a service is held and any new knights are installed. This is followed by lunch with the Queen in the Waterloo Chamber of Windsor Castle. There is a maximum of twenty-five Knights of this ancient and noble order that was founded by Edward III in 1349. Sir Edmund Hillary is one of them. He can usually be seen taking part in this annual ceremony in the full dress of a Garter Knight including the garter around the leg from which the Order takes its name. To get a ticket to watch the Garter procession write to: The Superintendent, Windsor Castle, Windsor, Berkshire SL4 1NJ.

It is particularly appropriate that the Queen should have elevated Hillary to this highest order of knighthood for he provided her – and the Empire – with a remarkable omen for a long and successful reign; the news that he, a member of the British Everset expedition, had become the first man to climb Mount Everest was received in London on the morning of the Coronation. Nobody gave the Queen a better Coronation gift than that.

Saint George's Chapel, the scene of Prince Edward's marriage to Sophie Rhys-Jones and of Princess Margaret's funeral, is one of the finest examples of Gothic architecture in Britain. Named after the patron saint of the Garter, it is the home of the Order.

In the Choir of the Chapel are the banners, crests, helmets and swords of each Knight. Sir Edmund Hillary's banner can be seen above his stall (seat) which is No. 16 on the right hand side as you face the altar. It shows mountains and three Nepalese prayer wheels to symbolise the gentle Hindu mountain kingdom where Mount Everset is situated. On his crest is a kiwi wielding an ice-axe and his supporters are Emperor penguins, recalling his exploration in the Antarctic. Other New Zealanders who have been Knights of the Garter were former Prime Minister, Sir Keith Holyoake, and distinguished airman, Lord Elworthy.

People are elevated to this most honourable of orders for their character and achievements. The only odd one out (and one which has caused a lot of controversy) is Emperor Akihito of Japan (Stall No. 14 on the left hand side facing the altar). In view of his refusal to apologise for the terrible war crimes that were committed in his father's name during the Second World War he is neither honourable nor decent. When he made his unwelcome and disastrous visit to Britain in 1998 he was met with passionate protests wherever he went. Never before had a State visitor been exposed to such hostility and there was much criticism when he was made a Knight of the Garter.

Also buried in Saint George's Chapel are three of the four kings who have reigned over New Zealand – Edward VII, George V and George VI. (The fourth king, Edward VIII who abdicated, is buried at Frogmore in the grounds of Windsor Castle). On the left side of the Chapel near the altar is a plaque in memory of the former Governor-General of New Zealand, Lord Freyberg V.C.

After he retired as Governor-General Freyberg was Deputy Constable and Lieutenant Governor of Windsor Castle from 1953 until his death in 1963 and he lived in the Norman Tower. Lord Elworthy from Timaru, the Chief of Defence Staff in Britain from 1967 to 1971, was Constable and Governor of the Castle from 1971 to 1978. He later retired to his family sheep station in South Canterbury. Lord Elworthy reached the highest rank in the Royal Air Force – that of Marshal of the Royal Air Force which is equivalent to Admiral of the Fleet or Field-Marshal in the two older services.

Saint George's Chapel is open to the public all year round apart from Sundays and during times of State visits.

In Windsor Great Park part of the Savill Gardens is planted as a New Zealand garden with native trees.

Runnymede

"At Runnymede, at Runnymede,
What say the reeds at Runnymede?
The lissom reeds that give and take,
That bend so far, but never break.
They keep the sleepy Thames awake
With tales of John at Runnymede....

You mustn't sell, delay, deny,
A freeman's right or liberty.
It wakes the stubborn Englishry,
We saw 'em roused at Runnymede!
And still when Mob or Monarch lays
Too rude a hand on English ways,
The whisper wakes, the shudder plays,
Across the reeds at Runnymede."

- Rudyard Kipling, *The Reeds of Runnymede*, 1911

Four miles east of Windsor is Runnymede (closest Station: Egham – from Waterloo). It was here on that historic Monday in June, 1215, that King John put his seal on Magna Carta, which was to be the basis of the rights and freedoms of all the peoples of the English speaking world – including, of course, New Zealanders.

The barons and churchmen were assembled on this meadow beside the Thames where a little throne had been erected for the king as well as a tent. The document which we know to-day as Magna Carta (Great Charter) had been drawn up on parchment to await the King's seal of approval.

Suddenly from the direction of the royal castle at Windsor could be seen a small and dusty cavalcade of galloping horses. They carried the King, the Papal Legate, the Archbishop of Canterbury and several bishops.

When they dismounted from their horses on the field of Runnymede the terms of the Charter were read to them and the King agreed. He put his seal on the document and returned to Windsor with all his churchmen. It is believed that the actual ceremony took place on the site which to-day is known as Magna Carta Island.

And what was so important about this document as to make it the foundation block of the rights and liberties that are enjoyed to-day by the sheep farmers of the Hawkes Bay, the factory workers of South Auckland, the pen pushers of Wellington and the fishermen of Bluff? Some of its articles are still relevant, e.g. Article 39 which established the important right of trial by jury and Article 42 which allows freedom of movement in and out of the country.

However, the true significance of Magna Carta was that it put an end to the arbitrary power of the Sovereign; henceforth the King must obey the law like everyone else. In other words, the supremacy of the law which is the system that we live under to-day. The earlier reign of Henry II had established the rule of law but the king was still above it. Magna Carta changed all that.

Whenever the State has tried to ride roughshod over the rights and liberties of the subject, it has been to Magna Carta, with its overwhelming principle that the sovereign power is bound by the law like everyone else, that appeal has been made and always successfully. That is why this small field beside the Thames has exercised such an enormous influence for good over the rights and freedoms of all the English speaking countries.

Also at this historic site is the Runnymede Memorial at the foot of Cooper's Hill which commemorates all the Air Force personnel who were killed in the Second World War and who have no known grave. This includes 583 New Zealanders who are commemorated on the monument.

The design of the memorial consists of a shrine with a cloister around it. The shape of the shrine is reminiscent of a wartime air-field control tower. It has a central arched opening, above which are three stone figures representing Justice, Victory and Courage.

The main feature of the shrine is its great north window on which are etched the words of the 139th Psalm, which is sometimes called the Airmen's Psalm. On each side of the words is an angel; above the head of each angel are engraved vapour trails that were taken from actual photographs of the sky during the Battle of Britain.

This magnificent window is the work of the renowned glass artist, John Hutton, an old boy of

Runnymede

Photograph: Commonwealth War Graves Commission
This etched window is the main feature of the shrine at the Runnymede Memorial which commemorates, among others, 583 New Zealand airmen who were killed in the Second World War and have no known grave. Designed by Wanganui Collegiate old boy, John Hutton, it looks over the field of Runnymede where King John signed Magna Carta, the foundation stone of the rights and freedoms of New Zealanders.

Wanganui Collegiate (See: Guildford and Coventry).
Hutton also created the painted ceilings of the shrine as well as the two look-outs from which on a clear day one can see six counties.

In the galleries around the quadrangle are columns which contain the names of the airmen. On the ceiling above are the arms of the Commonwealth countries – including New Zealand's. There is a Stone of Remembrance on the lawn. This moving memorial was unveiled by Her Majesty on 17th October, 1953. In her speech the Queen quoted the strangely prophetic words written by the poet, Alexander Pope, some two centuries earlier:

"On Cooper's Hill eternal wreaths shall grow

While lasts the mountain and while Thames doth flow".

The text of the speech can be read inside the covered gallery of the entrance. The Runnymede Memorial is open every day except Christmas Day. Hours: 9 a.m. – 6 p.m. on weekdays, 1st April-30th September and 10 a.m. – 6 p.m. on week-ends and public holidays. From 1st October to 31st March the times are 9 a.m. – 4 p.m. weekdays and 10 a.m. – 4 p.m. on week-ends and public holidays.

HAMPSHIRE

Emsworth

Just inside Hampshire on the A27 from Chichester in Sussex is Emsworth, a fishing town with some fine Georgian houses. It was here that New Zealand's greatest sailor, Sir Peter Blake, had his home.

Like Captain Cook, Blake was a great seaman whose violent death in a foreign land touched the whole world. His noble vision of cleaning up the world's oceans, which are being polluted every day by industrial companies and dirty municipalities, could only have come from a true son of the sea.

Sir Peter's funeral was held in the thousand year old church of Saint Thomas a'Becket at nearby Warblington and he is buried in its churchyard overlooking the sea that was both his life and his death. How appropriate that the church should be dedicated to Saint Thomas a'Becket who, like Blake, rose to the top of his calling and was then murdered in the execution of his duty – Becket inside Canterbury Cathedral and Blake on his boat, *Seamaster*.

Portsmouth

For several centuries Portsmouth has been one of the great naval ports of Britain and it was here that Captain Cook arrived on his ship, the *Resolution*, in July, 1775, after completing the second of his three voyages to the Pacific. The purpose of this trip had been to ascertain if the fabled great continent existed in the South Pacific and he was able to report that it didn't.

The most interesting part of Portsmouth for New Zealanders is the area around the naval base in Old Portsmouth. A good starting point is the city's leading attraction, *H.M.S.Victory*, which is docked at the Naval Base alongside the *Mary Rose*, the flagship of Henry VIII's fleet which was brought up from under the sea in 1982 and restored.

A few yards from Nelson's flagship is the Royal Naval Museum in which can be seen a model of the *Endeavour* as well as a section on how Captain Cook dealt successfully with the problem of scurvy among his crew.

Strongly recommended – especially for folk from Nelson! – is the "Trafalgar Experience", a fifteen minute multi-media production of the great sea battle where you can stand on the gun deck with the cannon going off all around. Hours: April-October, 10 a.m.- 5 p.m. November-March, 10 a.m.- 4.30 p.m.

From the Naval Base a short walk along the road known as The Hard and under the railway bridge into Saint George's Road will bring you to the High Street of Old Portsmouth. Turn right here (towards the sea) and a short distance down on the right is Portsmouth Cathedral.

In the Martyrs' Chapel, is a set of three beautiful stained glass windows. The highest of these is the D-Day Memorial window which contains the coats-of-arms of those nations whose troops took part in the

Normandy landings of June, 1944. The New Zealand crest is in the right hand column, third from the top.

Portsmouth was an important point of embarkation for the D-Day landings and General Eisenhower, the Supreme Commander, had his headquarters at Southwick House on the outskirts of the city.

In the days before the launching of this largest ever armada the Prime Minister of New Zealand, Peter Fraser, as well as Churchill and the other dominion Prime Ministers, visited the troops and inspected the operations.

From Portsmouth Cathedral a short walk down the High Street will bring you to the sea front. Take a left turn into Penny Street and you will see the ancient walls of the small Royal Garrison church.

Founded by a Crusader, Peter de Rupibus, Bishop of Winchester, in 1212, it was originally a hospice to provide accommodation for pilgrims from overseas who were on their way to the shrines of Canterbury, Chichester and Winchester.

In later years it served as the church for the army garrison at Portsmouth and in January, 1941, the nave was gutted during an enemy air-raid. Outside the church are various tombs; the large one on the right of the path leading to the church door is that of Sir Charles Napier (1782-1853), the conqueror of Sind in India after whom the city of Napier in the Hawkes Bay was named. (See: Trafalgar Square, London) The church is open Monday-Saturday, 11 a.m.- 4 p.m.

A short walk along Clarence Esplanade is the Royal Naval Memorial, a stone tower that overlooks the Solent. On the column are carved badges of the Royal Navy – Crown, Laurel, Wreath and Anchor. Like similar memorials at Chatham and Plymouth, it honours those men of the Royal Navy who were lost at sea in both world wars and have no known grave. Among the names are nine New Zealanders from the First World War – Burrows, Butler, Carpendale, Coney, Dalby, Follett, Green, Gully, and MacKay. The Memorial is accessible at all times and a service is held here on Remembrance Day, 11th November.

A short distance past the Naval Memorial and on a slight promontory overlooking the sea is Southsea Castle. A line across the sea from here to Spit Sand Fort used to be the starting point for the Whitbread Round-the-World yacht race; it was from here that Peter Blake and the crew of *Ceramco New Zealand* lined up at the start of the 1981-2 race in which they came second. The gun went off at noon. Next stop – Cape Town, 7,600 miles away.

Winchester

Winchester is a popular tourist destination for its magnificent Norman cathedral where Jane Austen is buried. Its Perpendicular nave is the longest in England and the second longest in Europe.

At Winchester's Peninsula Barracks is the museum of the Royal Green Jackets, which incorporates the old 43rd Light Infantry (the Monmouths) which fought at the battles of Gate Pa and Te Ranga in 1864 and at Okea in the Taranaki the following year

They built a redoubt at Tauranga in 1864 which is still there as the "Monmouth Redoubt"; nearby Monmouth Street is also named after this famous fighting regiment. In the museum can be seen a small display case about its role in the Maori War.

Southampton

This port city has always had important links with New Zealand. From its busy quays sailing ships took thousands of settlers to a new life in the Antipodes while in return its cool stores received thousands of tons of New Zealand farm produce in those secure and prosperous years before Britain joined the wretched European Common Market. People from Christchurch should feel particularly at home in Southampton since its suburbs have names like Shirley and Woolston.

South-east of the commercial centre and off Canute Road is the marina known as Ocean Village which is where the round-the-world yacht race starts and finishes. It was at the pontoon here at Ocean Village that Grant Dalton and the crew of *New Zealand Endeavour* sailed in with line honours to win the 1993-4 race that circumnavigated the globe.

Brockenhurst

South of Lyndhurst on the A337 is the town of Brockenhurst which was the site of the No. 1 New

Zealand General Hospital in the First World War to which New Zealand casualties from the Western Front were brought. It was set up in June, 1916, and took over Lady Hardinge's Hospital for the Indian troops of the Lahore and Meerut Divisions. This was named after Lady Hardinge, the wife of the then Viceroy of India.

This New Zealand hospital comprised several buildings including one on the Tile Barn site just south of the town and also the Forest Park Hotel (still there), which treated officers, and the Balmer Lawn Hotel in Lyndhurst Road. So great was the number of casualties that some of them were quartered in marquees on the lawns of the hotels.

When a soldier was wounded in France he was treated first at a field hospital and then, if necessary, sent to England for further treatment or recuperation. Most of the ships from France arrived at either Dover or Southampton; wounded New Zealanders who arrived at Dover were sent to the No.2 New Zealand General Hospital at Walton-on-Thames while those who reached Southampton were sent on by train to Brockenhurst. The last part of the journey for those who could not walk was by luggage trolley from Brockenhurst station to the hospital.

Besides tending the battle casualties the hospital also treated those with illnesses, the most common of which were trench fever, influenza and gas poisoning. There were almost three hundred nurses to staff the establishment and for the three years of its existence (1916-19) it treated 21,000 sick or wounded troops.

When it closed down at the beginning of 1919 the last cases were put on a hospital ship for home.

For those on the mend there was a recreation centre, known as the "Kia Ora Club"; it was situated in what is now the Masonic Hall. Football, cricket, hockey and golf teams were also formed.

At the time the population of Brockenhurst was less than 2,000 and the locals opened their homes and hearts to their kinsmen from across the sea. In fact, fourteen of the New Zealanders married local girls in the village church of Saint Nicholas in Church Lane, Brockenhurst.

Sadly that is not the only connection that the soldiers had with this country church deep in the heart of Hampshire; in its churchyard are the graves of ninety-three New Zealanders who died from either wounds or illness. Their graves are on the side of the hill and there is a Commonwealth War Graves Memorial in their honour. On the Sunday closest to Anzac Day an afternoon service is held at the Memorial to remember them.

After the War the relatives of those who died donated a bell for Saint Nicholas' church which is inscribed in memory of their loved ones.

Inside the church can be seen a letter that was written by the Officer Commanding to the vicar, thanking the people of Brockenhurst for their kindness and hospitality. Also in the church is a New Zealand corner which has a Roll of Honour and commemorative plaque; there is also a national flag. A little piece of New Zealand in Hampshire.

DORSET

Christchurch

The town of Christchurch, just east of Bournemouth on the south coast of Dorset, is a sister city of its namesake on the Canterbury Plains. This is due to their having the same names but it is important to remember that Christchurch, New Zealand, was not named after Christchurch, Dorset, but in honour of Christ Church College, Oxford, where many of the founders of the Canterbury settlement, including its leader, John Robert Godley, were educated.

Christchurch, Dorset, has a population of 44,000 and is a centre for windsurfing. Just as Christchurch, New Zealand, is dominated by its Cathedral so too is the eleventh century Priory church, with its great Norman nave, an important feature of Christchurch, Dorset. And both towns have a River Avon flowing through them but, as with the towns themselves, the names have separate origins. In Christchurch's Alice in Wonderland Family Park is the largest maze in southern England.

Southwell on the Isle of Portland

The southernmost village in Dorset is Southwell on the Isle of Portland, south of Weymouth. In Avalanche Road, Southwell, is a tiny church that was built in memory of those who lost their lives when the three masted clipper, *Avalanche*, sank off Portland Bill, which is less than a mile from the church, on the dark evening of 11th September, 1877. She was on her way to New Zealand with emigrants when she was hit by a larger vessel, the *Forest*. Ninety-four of the *Avalanche's* ninety-seven passengers and crew were drowned in the cold ocean.

The church contains some interesting mementoes of this ship that didn't make it to New Zealand. There is a model of the vessel and some artefacts that were recovered from the wreck, including one of its anchors. Viewing of the church and its salvaged artefacts can be arranged by ringing (01305) 821-390.

The south Auckland suburb of Weymouth on the Manukau harbour is named after Weymouth in Dorset.

WILTSHIRE

Codford Saint Mary

During the First World War this was the site of the No. 3 New Zealand General Hospital. In the New Churchyard of the village church of Saint Mary are the graves of sixty-six New Zealand soldiers of the First World War who died of sickness or from their wounds.

Bulford, near Stonehenge

Taking the A3028, which leads off the A303 west of Andover, one comes to the village of Bulford. During the First World War this was the site of a huge army estate that was known as Sling Camp. It was the centre for training reinforcements for the New Zealand forces in France and Flanders. At the end of the War some 4,500 New Zealand soldiers were stationed here. Described by New Zealand's Official War Historian as "unloved, bleak and lonely", Sling was on the edge of Salisbury Plain, the 92,000 acre British Army base where more ammunition can be fired on one day than would be fired by the whole New Zealand Army in a year. It had its own "Kiwi Barracks" and to-day the local school is called Kiwi School. Bulford is presently the base for the British Army's 249 Signal Squadron.

The hills around here are made of chalk and the area is well-known for the *Giant Man, White Horse* and other prehistoric chalk figures that are carved on its hilltops.

After the War there were not enough troopships to take all the New Zealanders home at once and the ones who had to wait out their time here at Sling grew very bored. There was trouble. Even though the War was over, the authorities did not relax the discipline and one night the troops decided that they had had enough and they went on the rampage, looting the canteen and officers' mess and drinking all that they found.

So as to channel their youthful energy into something more constructive than raiding drinks cabinets, one of the more enlightened colonels suggested that they add to the great prehistoric chalk figures by making a giant kiwi out of chalk on the hill above the camp.

He arranged for the engineers to tape out the outlines while the original drawing was done from a sketch in the British Museum by Sergeant Major Percy Blenkarne, a drawing instructor with the New Zealand Division.

Thus it was that the 420 foot high kiwi, with its 150 foot long beak, was dug out of the gentle slope of Beacon Hill above the camp by men (mostly engineers) of the Canterbury Battalion in February and March, 1919. The kiwi is flanked by 65 foot high letters "N.Z".

Working in four hour shifts, forty men at a time, the soldiers removed twelve inches of topsoil with pick and shovel and then came the time to fill it with chalk. Unfortunately the chalk in the immediate vicinity was pink and that would never do so they quarried white chalk from a spot four hundred yards further down and carried it up in sandbags like Chinese coolies – more than 10,000 bags in all. And that is how the giant kiwi joined the other figures that were made thousands of years earlier.

After the troops returned to New Zealand their work of art was maintained for three decades by the Kiwi Boot Polish Company in order to promote its label and then by local volunteers and finally by British troops who in 1980 completely restored the carving with nearly 100 tons of fresh chalk. During the Second World War Big Kiwi was covered over so as not to give the Luftwaffe a landmark indication of the site of Bulford camp.

On Beacon Hill is a plaque mounted on a cairn that commemorates the world's largest kiwi carved in chalk.

Every year the 249 Signal Squadron holds a March and Shoot competition called the Kiwi Trophy and the winner is presented with a carved wooden model of a kiwi which was presented by the New Zealand Army in 1981. The soldiers have to march fourteen miles with 30 lb of weight on their backs. During the march they must fire ten shots on the range with each dropped shot incurring a penalty. The winner usually completes the course in approximately two and a half hours.

A mile east of Bulford on the A303 is its junction with the A338. Turn left here and follow the sign to Marlborough; about a mile further on is the Tidworth Military Cemetery where 102 New Zealand soldiers are buried, most of them victims of the Spanish flu that swept the world at the end of the First World War.

DEVON

Ashburton

On the south-eastern side of Dartmoor is the quaint town of Ashburton which dates back to the Middle Ages. It is just off the Exeter-Plymouth motorway (A38) and has a "twin" relationship with the town of Ashburton on the Canterbury Plains which was named after Hon. Francis Baring, the third Lord Ashburton and a member of the Canterbury Association. Its many slate hung buildings give it a slightly medieval atmosphere.

Torquay

Best known as the setting for *Fawlty Towers*, Torquay has another and deeper meaning for New Zealanders. On the road leading to Barton is Torquay Cemetery. In the south-west section of the original cemetery is a small group of seven graves of New Zealand soldiers from the First World War. They are situated opposite the other World War One graves.

The town of Torquay looks over Tor Bay, after which Torbay and Torbay Heights on the north shore of Auckland are named.

Dartmouth

Both Dartmoor and Dartmouth are named after the River Dart, the town of Dartmouth, of course, being at the river's mouth. It is best known for its Royal Naval College where quite a few of New Zealand's naval officers have received their training over the years. So perhaps it is not surprising to find that one of its streets, that contains the museum, is called Anzac Street.

Plymouth

One of the most noticeable traits of New Zealanders is their love of the sea – be it the Auckland Anniversary Regatta, the America's Cup, the long distance swimming of Cook Strait or the thousands of surfers who go out in all weathers to catch their waves. It is interesting to note that this link with the sea was established at the very beginning and by none other than the greatest navigator the world has ever known. And it all started when Captain Cook sailed out of Plymouth Hoe on a voyage that was to change the world. It is for this reason that Plymouth has a special place in the New Zealand story just as it has for the United States since it was from here that the *Mayflower* sailed to Massachusetts in 1620. By virtue of its geographical position, Plymouth is the last major British port for ships setting out on the Seven Seas and a wander around its old harbour, known as The Barbican, is like a trip down Memory Lane.

It was from here that Captain Cook set out on his three voyages to the Pacific. He left Plymouth Harbour on 25th August, 1768, on the *Endeavour* which had a crew of 94 men. It was on this voyage that he discovered and charted New Zealand, giving it many of the place names with which we are familiar to-day – Poverty Bay, Bay of Plenty, Mercury Bay, Mount Egmont, Queen Charlotte Sound, Banks Peninsula, Cape Foulwind, Cape Kidnappers and Dusky Sound.

It was while he and his crew were anchored at Ship Cove in Queen Charlotte Sound that he took possession of New Zealand "in the name and for the use of His Majesty" who, of course, was George III. They then drank a toast to the health of the Queen, Charlotte, (after whom the Sound was named) and the empty wine bottle was given to an old Maori. With his usual prescience Cook wrote in his diary, "Was this Country (New Zealand) settled by an Industrus people, they would very soon be supply'd not only with the necessarys but many of the luxuries of life."

Cook and his men enjoyed their stay at Ship Cove. "In the morning," he wrote, "we were awakened by the singing of the birds. The number was incredible, and they seemed to strain their throats in emulation of each other. This wild melody was infinitely superior to anything that we have ever heard of the kind; it seemed to be like small bells most exquisitely attuned."

Cook also sailed from Plymouth on the *Resolution* (462 tons) on 13th July, 1772, when he went in search of the imaginary southern continent, which he was able to report did not exist. On this voyage he again put into Ship Cove as indeed he did on his last and fatal journey of 1776-7, which also left from Plymouth – the last piece of England that Captain Cook ever saw.

This was also the port from which the first settlers left to found the settlement of New Plymouth in 1840.

In January of that year a public meeting was held in Plymouth for the purpose of forming a company, the Plymouth Company, with the specific purpose of colonising New Zealand with people from the south-west of England. The head of the company was the Earl of Devon; thus the town was named New Plymouth and its main thoroughfare, Devon Street.

After purchasing 60,000 acres of land in Taranaki from the New Zealand Company the Plymouth Company sent out the first settlers on 19th November, 1840, on board the *William Bryan*.

The ship reached the site of New Plymouth in March, 1841, and in the next two years another five sailing vessels, carrying almost a thousand settlers, followed. New Plymouth was under way.

It was the arrival of these settlers and the establishment of the town of New Plymouth that brought some much needed law and order to the Taranaki and enabled its former Maori inhabitants to return. In 1823 the area had been almost entirely depopulated when a Waikato tribe marauded through the area, killing many of the local Maoris and forcing the rest to flee to Kapiti and the Marlborough Sounds. It was only the arrival of the European colonists and their establishment of a settlement that enabled the Taranaki Maoris to return. At the old harbour of Plymouth and only a few yards from the Mayflower Steps, over which the American and British flags fly, is a memorial to the brave band of West Country settlers who sailed from this ancient port to colonise the Taranaki.

Also at the Barbican is a memorial to the *Tory* which sailed from Plymouth on 12th May, 1839 to found the settlement of Wellington. Those on board were mostly officials of the New Zealand Company; they were the "advance guard" whose task was to choose the site of the settlement and prepare it for the passenger ships which would follow.

In command of this 382 ton barque was Captain Edward Chaffers, after whom Wellington's Chaffers passage and Chaffers marina are named. The First Mate was Richard Lowry, who gave his name to Lowry Bay while the Surgeon was Doctor John Dorset, after whom Fort Dorset was named. Also on board were Colonel William Wakefield, the Resident-General of the New Zealand Company and his nephew, Edward Jerningham Wakefield whose name is commemorated at Wellington's Point Jerningham where twenty-one gun salutes are fired on royal birthdays.

Plymouth was also the last port-of-call in England for the First Four Ships of the Canterbury settlement which sailed out of Plymouth harbour in September, 1850, on their way to a great adventure and a great achievement.

All these founding colonists brought not only themselves and their possessions but also their Christian religion, the English language, Parliamentary institutions and centuries of traditions like Guy Fawkes, field sports and roast beef and Yorkshire pudding on Sundays. Like the oak tree and the rabbit, these flourished in the new land and forged its character.

The visitor will have noticed that the commercial centre of Plymouth is mostly post-war concrete and glass; this is because, as an important naval port, Plymouth was heavily bombed by the Germans; at the end of April, 1941, the city suffered five air raids in nine nights. By 1945 the centre of the city was one huge bomb site.

Fortunately, the area around the Barbican emerged largely unscathed and so, by looking around at the narrow lanes, old stone buildings and quaint dockside pubs, one is able to get some idea of the sight that the emigrants got as they said their good-byes on shore and were rowed out to the waiting sailing ship for the long voyage to the Antipodes.

In the park on Plymouth Hoe, from where Sir Francis Drake sailed out to defeat the Spanish Armada in 1588 after finishing his game of bowls, is the fine Naval Memorial to those sailors who were killed at sea during the two world wars and who have no known grave.

After the First World War it was decided to honour these men with three similar memorials – at Chatham in Kent, Portsmouth in Hampshire, and here at Plymouth for these were the three main ports in Britain from which the naval vessels set out.

The memorial is a tower of Portland stone, supported by four corner buttresses, each with a lion couchant. At the top the tower branches out into four ships' prows and above them are representations of the four winds, which support a large copper sphere symbolising the globe of the world. The base contains bronze panels that record the names of the dead. These include Auckland born William Sanders who won the Victoria Cross for an action when he was serving on *H.M.S.Prize* in the Atlantic in 1917. A few months later he was killed at sea off Ireland. The Sanders Cup, New Zealand's premier sailing trophy, is named after him.

At the end of the Second World War a sunken sheltered garden was created to accommodate the names of all those who died at sea between 1939 and 1945 and this is a truly tranquil and poignant place to spend a few reflective moments.

Two miles north-east from the centre of Plymouth on Efford Road is the Plymouth Efford Cemetery which contains the graves of twenty-two New Zealand soldiers of the First World War, most of whom died in Plymouth hospitals – either from the wounds they suffered in France or from sickness.

The cemetery also has a memorial to more than a thousand Plymouth civilians who were killed in German air raids during the Second World War – a grim reminder of the battering that this naval port took at the hands of the Luftwaffe. Each evening buses evacuated women and children to nearby villages while those for whom there was no room on the buses walked out of the city with their children and belongings in prams.

West of the city of Plymouth is the naval base of Devonport from where the ferry crosses the Tamar River to Torpoint. Because of its early naval associations Devonport on the north shore of Auckland was named after Devonport on the Tamar.

Bere Ferrers

This tiny village, north of Plymouth and on the other side of the River Tavy, was the scene of a tragedy for some New Zealand soldiers of the First World War.

Having just arrived in England, they were put on a train and told that there would be a refreshment stop at Exeter. The train pulled up for a moment at Bere Ferrers and some of them, in the mistaken belief that they had reached Exeter, opened the doors and got out. They stepped on to the adjacent track and were hit by an oncoming train. Ten of them were killed. There is a plaque in their memory in the local church of Saint Andrew's and in November, 2001, their names were added to the Bere Ferrers war memorial.

CORNWALL

In no other English county are they as keen on rugby as in Cornwall. This, coupled with its long coastline, crashing surf, green fields and slightly "colonial" atmosphere, should make the New Zealand traveller feel very much at home.

Torpoint

Just across the River Tamar from Plymouth is the Tudor mansion of Mount Edgcumbe House and its lovely park from which there are wonderful views over Plymouth Sound to Dartmoor. The house, which was the home of the Mount Edgcumbe family for four centuries, has been restored after it was gutted by a German incendiary bomb in 1941 and is now in public ownership. Inside can be seen family treasures, paintings by Reynolds and van der Velde, Bronze Age horns, sixteenth century tapestries and eighteenth century porcelain.

The present Earl of Mount Edgcumbe, who inherited the title and the estate in 1982, was formerly a farm manager for the Lands and Survey Department in New Zealand. The earl divides his time between his New Zealand home in Otorohonga and Cornwall. However, when in England he does not stay at Mount Edgcumbe House but at Empacombe House near Cremyll, the village from which one enters Mount Edgcumbe Park.

And how is it that a gentleman from Otorohonga holds a higher position in the aristocracy than any other New Zealander? The story is as follows. A certain Edward Mortimer, who was the nephew of the 3rd Earl of Mount Edgcumbe, emigrated to New Zealand during the Maori War and served as a Justice of the Peace and Lieutenant in the Militia. His son, George, married a New Zealand girl, Georgina Bell, and their son, Edward, inherited the title as the 7th Earl of Mount Edgcumbe. When he died in 1982 the title passed to his son, Robert, the present Earl.

The 800 acres of Mount Edgcumbe Park stretch along ten miles of spectacular coast from Cremyll to Whitsand Bay. From this promontory the ancestors of the present earl looked out at the Spanish Armada and to-day there are various vantage points such as

Thomson's Seat, Milton's Temple, the Folly and the Arch, from which are breathtaking views over sea and land. There is a special plantation of New Zealand trees in the New Zealand Garden which was planted in 1989 to commemorate the family links with the land which now produces the Earls. The native plants – cabbage tree, kowhai, ti tree, kaka beak, rata, flax, fern and other species - thrive here in the mild Cornish climate. They are planted around a geyser – shades of Rotorua! Grazing among the trees in the Park are wild fallow deer and there are fortifications that date from the Iron Age.

Another feature of Mount Edgcumbe Park is the National Camellia Collection; they usually flower between February and April. There is also an English Garden as well as an American Garden, an Italian Garden and a French Garden – all reflecting the styles of their country of origin.

One can reach Mount Edgcumbe by ferry from Plymouth (Stonehouse) which arrives at the entrance to the park. The House is open from the beginning of April to the end of September, Wednesdays –Sundays as well as on Bank Holidays. Hours: 11 a.m.- 4.30 p.m. The Park is open every day of the year and is free.

Looe

The picturesque seaside village of Looe on the Channel coast of Cornwall has an interesting association with New Zealand's most famous writer. Katherine Mansfield lived there for several months in

1918 shortly after her marriage to John Middleton Murry. In an attempt to regain her health she stayed at the Headland Hotel which she described as "a perfect sanatorium". In a letter to her husband she wrote, "The approach to Looe is amazing....We drove through lanes like great flowering loops with sea below and huge gulls sailing over....You shall have strawberries, love in this happy land, three times a day...Picnics! We shall have almost perpetual picnics".

When her husband joined her, they went to the local pub and beauty spots. While at Looe she worked on *Bliss and Other Stories*, which were set in New Zealand. Maybe the cliffs and beaches reminded her of home.

Bodmin

The many links between New Zealand and the south-west county of Cornwall go right back to the very beginning. When the New Zealand Company's ship, the *Tory*, sailed into Wellington Harbour filled with hopeful settlers on 20th September, 1839, Colonel William Wakefield, the brother of Edward Gibbon Wakefield and the Resident-General of the Company in New Zealand, named the cape on the east of the harbour entrance "Pencarrow" after the family seat in Cornwall of Sir William Molesworth, who was a director of the New Zealand Company. Wellington's Molesworth Street, near Parliament, was also named after him.

Pencarrow is situated just north of the village of Washaway off the A389. Washaway itself is three and a half miles north of Bodmin. Pencarrow has been the ancestral home of the Molesworth-Saint Aubyn family since the sixteenth century. Besides being a director of the New Zealand Company as well as Secretary of State for the Colonies, Sir William Molesworth also found time to create what is one of the most beautiful gardens in England.

He began this task when he was twenty-one and continued it for the next fifty years. Some of the plants were sent to him from New Zealand by his brother, Francis, in the 1840s including the New Zealand fuschia (excorticata), rama-rama (Myrtus bullata), the red parrot's bill (Clianthus puniceus), totara and karaka.

The Georgian house at Pencarrow has an excellent collection of eighteenth century paintings, furniture and porcelain and there are tearooms and a craft centre in the grounds. It is open to the public during the summer.

Several Cornish gentlemen were associated with the New Zealand Company in the beginning including Captain Lawrence, R.N., Captain Daniell and Lord Vivian, all of whom have Wellington streets named after them, and Lord Petre who was associated with the founding of Wanganui. And quite a few of Wellington's early settlers were Cornish. In the first settlement at Petone there was even a street known as Cornish Row – a long line of reed and flax cottages belonging to about forty settlers from Cornwall. Unfortunately they all went up in flames on 25th May, 1840, and the fire was followed by an earthquake – a strange reversal of the usual order!

Falmouth

Situated even closer to the sea routes of the world than Plymouth, Falmouth was often the last port-of-call for sailing ships that left from London, Southampton and other places. If a vessel had a rough passage down the Channel, she would put into Falmouth for repairs and replenishment – especially water. On days when great gales raged at sea as many as four hundred sailing vessels would sprout a forest of masts in the sheltered waters of Falmouth harbour. It was also the first port-of-call for the wool clippers bringing Australian and New Zealand wool to Britain.

Until 1850 Falmouth was the base for the overseas mail service and the ships that carried the letters and parcels from here to New Zealand and other parts of the world were called the "Falmouth Packets"; in fact, the local newspaper still bears the salty title of the *Falmouth Packet*.

Because of the depressed conditions in the local tin mines in the nineteenth century thousands of Cornish miners and their families left from here to make a new life in New Zealand where they applied their skills on the goldfields of the West Coast, Otago, Thames, Coromandel and elsewhere. In the early 1840s ships such as *the Regina, Timandra, West Briton* and *Blenheim* arrived in Auckland and Wellington full of Cornish settlers and their families.

Falmouth played host to the men of the New Zealand Tunnelling Corps who sailed into Plymouth harbour on board the *Ruapehu* on 3rd February, 1916.

The Tunnelling Corps was raised because of the particular nature of trench warfare on the Western Front. The military tunnels were hand dug with a pick axe and the earth was then carried out in sand bags. They drove the tunnels out beneath no-man's land and then exploded mines under the German trenches and launched surprise attacks using concealed exits. Many of the men who enlisted in the Tunnelling Corps had worked on the Otira Tunnel which was then being dug under the Southern Alps to link Westland with Canterbury and which employed an estimated 60,000 men during the fifteen years of its construction.

After disembarking in Plymouth the 16 officers and 407 other ranks of the Tunnelling Corps took the train to Falmouth. Fresh in the Home Country after eight weeks at sea these virile and excited young men chatted up every woman on the train.

Upon arrival in Falmouth they were met by several bands as well as a civic dinner with lots of beer. It was pouring with rain by the time the men made their way up to the camp on the Hornwork, the picturesque promontory crowned by Pendennis Castle which overlooks the harbour. The castle, built by Henry VIII with the money he got from selling the monasteries, guards the entrance to the harbour. It is so strong that during the Civil War it took the Parliamentary forces five months to reduce it by siege. It is open to the public and is reached by Castle Drive which winds its way up the hill.

From the ramparts of the castle there is a wonderful view of the Falmouth peninsula including the old town and harbour. Close your eyes and try to imagine a Falmouth Packet setting out in full sail bound for distant New Zealand with the eagerly awaited mail from Home.

The troops were housed in huts as they carried out their month's training for the beaver like work that awaited them near Flanders. Before they were sent to the Front they were given a few days' leave to see something of Britain. On the eve of their departure they were inspected by Sir Thomas McKenzie, the New Zealand High Commissioner in London, who read out a message from Lord Kitchener, "Please give my best wishes to the New Zealanders and say I am sure they will worthily uphold Anzac traditions".

At midnight on 7th March, 1916, the Tunnelling Corps caught the train for Southampton en route for the killing fields of France and Belgium, the "faithful Fusiliers band with half the female population of the county giving it a touching farewell".

It was a freezing night and, when the train reached Exeter at 4 a.m., the local ladies had set up tables on the snow covered platform to serve hot drinks and food to the Tunnellers.

SOMERSET

Wellington

A few miles north of Taunton and just off the M5 is the market town of Wellington which gave its name to New Zealand's capital city in an indirect and somewhat haphazard way. When Arthur Wellesley and his army defeated the French in the Battle of Talavera during the Peninsular War he was elevated to the peerage and he had to take the title of his viscountcy from a particular place. Since he was in the mountains of Portugal with his army and the College of Heralds was pressing for a decision, his brother, William, chose the town of Wellington in Somerset because it was not far from Welleslie from where the family took their name. When he heard of his brother's decision the new Viscount Wellington (later to become Duke) was delighted – "I think you have chosen most fortunately", he wrote. And that is how Arthur Wellesley became the Duke of Wellington and gave his name to New Zealand's capital city.

On the hill above Wellington, Somerset, is an obelisk in honour of the Iron Duke. Hills and Wellington? They always seem to go together; even the maiden name of Wellington's mother was Hill!

Bath

The ancient and picturesque city of Bath is famous for its great Abbey, its Roman Baths and its round avenue of fine Georgian houses known as The Circus. It is of particular historical interest to people from the Hawkes Bay because it was the home of two great soldiers whose names were given to Hawkes Bay towns.

Outside No. 14 The Circus is a plaque in honour of Robert Clive ("Clive of India"), who used to live here (See: Whitehall and Westminster, London) while on the wall of No. 9 Henrietta Street is a similar plaque recording the residence here of General Sir Charles Napier (See: Trafalgar Square, London).

GLOUCESTERSHIRE

Lydney

On the western side of the Severn River is Lydney. West of the town and just off the A48 is Lydney Park, the home of the Bledisloe family. Lord Bledisloe was Governor-General of New Zealand from 1930 to 1935; he is widely regarded as the best and most popular Governor-General that New Zealand has ever had (See: The Temple, London, and Oxford).

In the grounds of Lydney Park is a Roman temple site and a museum with Roman exhibits. There is also a New Zealand Museum containing some of the things that Lord Bledisloe was presented with during his vice-regal term. He for his part presented the Treaty House at Waitangi and its grounds to the nation.

In the New Zealand Museum can be seen large samples of amber resin and other colourful mineral extracts, shells, teeth and jaws of large fish, Maori artefacts, engraved silver trowels that were presented to the Governor when he opened bridges, roads, etc. and some fine embellished books, some of which have beautiful original water-colours of New Zealand scenes. There is a book from the Masonic Lodges of New Zealand and another from the City of Auckland as well as others. Covers are made of leather or native wood and the books are in presentation boxes.

The grounds of Lydney include a deer park where one can have a picnic. Lydney Park is open from 11 a.m. to 6 p.m. on Sundays, Wednesdays and Bank Holiday Mondays from 24th March to 9th June. Group and guided tours can be arranged on any day during this period – Tel: (01594) 845497. Teas can be had in the dining room of the Mansion, the only room of the house that is open to the public.

Gloucester

This ancient cathedral city was known to the Romans and pieces of a statue of a Roman emperor were uncovered by archaeologists. As a millennium project it was decided to re-create the bronze statue on the site of the original. The sculptor chosen for this important work was British born Anthony Stones, who lived in New Zealand from 1952 to 1983 and has been responsible for crafting several fine statues in New Zealand. (See: Greenwich, London, and Derby)

Daylesford

Daylesford, a small hamlet south of Stratford-upon-Avon and east of Cheltenham, was the ancestral home of the family of Warren Hastings who gave his name to the city of Hastings in the Hawkes Bay.

The Hastings family were once great landowners but they lost their fortune during Cromwell's wars and had to sell the family home here in Daylesford. As a child Warren dreamed of winning it back. His mother died when he was young and he was brought up by an uncle. At the age of sixteen he went out to India to serve in the East India Company.

Rising through the ranks Hastings became Governor of Bengal in 1772. When the administration was unified he was appointed the first Governor-General of India and saw off a major French threat to the sub-continent. He also fought against corruption in the East India Company but this upset certain people in England; upon his return they tried to impeach him.

After a trial that lasted seven years they were unable to prove a single charge against this great and honourable man; in fact, so disreputable was the prosecution of these bogus charges that never again has an impeachment been attempted in Britain or the Commonwealth. We leave that sort of thing to the Americans and look on as they tear their nation apart in the process.

Warren Hastings realised his boyhood dream and bought back the family home here in Daylesford. His grave can be seen in the local churchyard.

Daylesford is a couple of miles east of Chipping Norton and a short distance off the A436.

HERTFORDSHIRE

Saint Albans

The cathedral town of Saint Alban's, twenty-one miles north of London, was founded by the Romans who called in Verulamium after the river Ver which flows through the town. It acquired its present name from the first man to die for the Christian faith in Britain, a Roman soldier stationed at Verulamium who was called Alban. His name is also honoured in New Zealand by the Christchurch suburb of Saint Albans. The tower of Saint Alban's cathedral was constructed in the twelfth century out of bricks and tiles from the old Roman settlement of Verulamium.

Saint Albans is the venue for an annual Anzac service which takes place on the afternoon of the Sunday closest to Anzac Day at Hatfield Road Cemetery where several Australian and Canadian war dead are buried.

CAMBRIDGESHIRE

Cambridge

Tota illa Atrata ex cohors

- Part of the Latin address in honour of Peter Fraser, Prime Minister of New Zealand, when he was awarded an honorary Ll.D degree by Cambridge University in May, 1944. It is probably the only attempt ever to describe the All Blacks in Latin. A literal translation is "All that black-robed company".

"The great glory of Cambridge's beauty is the river and its surroundings," wrote the New Zealand author, Alan Mulgan. "To go up the river on a fine summer afternoon when it is crowded with gaily dressed young people…..to pass by these exquisite old buildings and their walled gardens, to land and wander under the trees over velvet lawns, is one of the most delightful experiences to be found in England."

There is no reason to dispute any of Mulgan's words for indeed a cruise on a punt past the college buildings, so many of them architectural gems that rise straight out of the water, and the willows and manicured lawns that enclose them is to absorb something of the soul of this ancient seat of learning. However, for the sake of convenience we are going to explore these colleges, where quite a few New

Zealanders have been privileged to study, by wandering through its narrow, bicycle strewn lanes.

Every student at Cambridge (and Oxford) is a member of both his or her college and the university. By having their students living in a college, dining formally in black gowns with their fellow students in the college's Great Hall, and taking part in the myriad sporting and cultural activities that are available, Cambridge and Oxford tend to civilise their students as well as educate them. It is this that gives the two universities their unrivalled prestige. In this crude and vulgar age of "egalitarianism" they remain havens of excellence, beauty and civility.

We will begin our tour of this world famous seat of learning at the northern end of the town; Magdalene College (pronounced "Maudlin") is at the end of Bridge Street, on the left bank of the river over the Great Bridge. Among those who have studied at this small and pleasant college was Samuel Marsden (1765-1838), the missionary who performed the first Christian service in New Zealand on Christmas Day, 1814. He was at Magdalene in 1790 but was persuaded by William Wilberforce, the anti-slavery campaigner, to cut short his studies and carry the gospel to Australia.

Marsden became chaplain to the convict settlement of New South Wales and also a magistrate where the excessive sentences of corporal punishment that he imposed on wrongdoers led to his nickname "The Flogging Parson". From Sydney he made several trips to New Zealand to convert the Maoris to Christianity but without much success. Marsden Point on Bream Bay, North Auckland, and the Samuel Marsden Collegiate school for girls in Wellington are named after him.

Next to Magdalene is Saint John's College. Situated on both banks of the River Cam, its two parts are joined by the beautiful Bridge of Sighs. Saint John's has several links with the founding of New Zealand. George Augustus Selwyn, the Etonian who became the first Bishop of New Zealand, read classics here before entering the Church. He later had the rare distinction of having a Cambridge college named after him – Selwyn College (at the other end of Cambridge and across the river), which was founded for the purpose of providing a university education for practising members of the Church of England.

While serving in New Zealand as its first bishop between 1842 and 1868, Selwyn also founded Saint John's theological college, which he named after his old college in Cambridge. Established first at Waimate North, Saint John's was later moved to Auckland. The Selwyn River in Canterbury is named after him while the white stone pulpit in Christchurch Cathedral is dedicated to his memory.

From Saint John's – as from other colleges – it is a common sight to see oarsmen on the river. Each college has its crew and the best are selected for the Cambridge Eight who row against Oxford in the Boat Race that takes place each April on the Thames at Putney. In fact, New Zealand's connection with this famous event goes right back to the inaugural Boat

Race of 1829 when Selwyn, the future Bishop of New Zealand, rowed in the Cambridge Eight.

Another link that Saint John's College has with early New Zealand is Samuel Butler who arrived at Lyttelton in 1860 and explored the mountain headwaters of four of Canterbury's rivers and was the first man to discover and cross the Whitcombe Pass in 1861. Butler then established a huge sheep run, Mesopatamia, which eventually comprised 55,000 acres. The grandeur of the mountains and plains and the solitude of life on a remote sheep station led him to write *A First Year in the Canterbury Settlement* in 1863 and later *Erewhon* which, with one alteration, is the word "Nowhere" spelt backwards. In *Erewhon* Butler portrays the beauty of the New Zealand landscape.

Butler rode on the footplate of the first train to run in New Zealand – between Christchurch and Ferrymead in 1863. Although he returned to Britain the following year his name is commemorated in the South Island by Mount Butler, the Butler Range and the Butler Saddle. While here at Saint John's in Cambridge Butler took a degree in classics and was a coxswain and coach for the Cambridge Eight.

Sir Francis Dillon Bell, the first New Zealand born Prime Minister and a relation of Edward Gibbon Wakefield, was also educated at Saint John's, graduating in mathematics. When William Massey died in 1925, Bell became caretaker Prime Minister for a short time until the Reform Party elected Gordon Coates to take over.

Next to Saint John's is Trinity College. Founded by King Henry VIII in 1546, this is the largest of the colleges that make up Cambridge University while its Library, designed by Sir Christopher Wren, is regarded as the second most beautiful building in Cambridge after King's College Chapel. Among its alumni have been the great mathematician who defined the law of gravity, Sir Isaac Newton, the poets Tennyson and Byron, the current Prince of Wales and New Zealand's greatest tennis player, Anthony Wilding who had his rooms in Trinity's New Court. Besides taking his law degree Wilding also represented Trinity at both rugby and cricket. In that civilised and relaxed age the hours between 2 p.m. and 4.30 p.m. were for games. In Wilding's words, those are "the worst hours in the day for work and the best for play". In his first year he won the Freshman's tennis tournament and was in the Cambridge University team that played Oxford in 1904 and 1905. He was both captain and Honorary Secretary of the Cambridge University Lawn Tennis Club. After leaving Cambridge Wilding won the Wimbledon Men's Singles Championship four years in a row (1910-13). This world famous sporting gentleman was killed in the First World War. Wilding Park, the headquarters of tennis in his home town of Christchurch, is named after him.

Another Trinity man whose name is perpetuated in a Christchurch place name is Samuel Bealey (1821-1909), the third Superintendent of Canterbury, after whom Christchurch's Bealey Avenue is named as well as the Bealey River and the town of Bealey in the

Southern Alps. He took his B.A. at Trinity in 1851 and emigrated to Canterbury a few months later.

Three generations of Elworthys from South Canterbury, including Lord Elworthy, who was Chief of Defence Staff in Britain from 1967 to 1971, have gone to Trinity and in the process have picked up several rowing Blues. Lord Cobham, Governor-General from 1957 to 1962, was also a Trinity man who did a law degree.

Adjacent to Trinity and down by the river is Clare College. Situated in the centre of the cluster of colleges and overlooking both the River Cam and the Lawn of King's, Clare was originally called Clare Hall. It was founded in 1326 by Elizabeth de Burgh, widow of the Earl of Clare and grand-daughter of Edward I. Part of her purpose in founding it was to educate young men so that they could replace those who had been wiped out by the Black Death. Even plagues have their good consequences! None of the original medieval buildings survive; they were all burned down and replaced by one of the most beautiful college buildings in Cambridge; in its appearance it could well be a Renaissance palace. Lord Cooke of Thorndon, the former President of the New Zealand Court of Appeal, did his M.A. and Ph.D. at Clare College and is now a Fellow of Gonville and Caius College. (Caius is pronounced "Keys") A Fellow of an Oxford or Cambridge college is someone who has taken a Bachelor of Arts or some higher degree and has been elected to a fellowship with a view to teaching or research at the college. He also sits at the Fellows'

(High) table in the college Hall. One is normally elected a Fellow for three years. A college consists of its Master, Fellows and scholars. Since every peer must have a place in Britain as part of his title, Lord Cooke chose Cambridge; his full title is Lord Cooke of Thorndon in New Zealand and of the County of Cambridgeshire.

The great Lawn of King's, next to Clare, is dominated by King's College Chapel. This magnificent example of the Perpendicular style of the fifteenth century is one of the most beautiful buildings in the world. Apart from York Minster it is the only major medieval church still to have its original windows. King's College was founded by Henry VI in 1441.

On the other side of King's Parade turn into Bene't Street and then right into Free School Lane. On the east side of this short street is a plaque recording that this was the site until 1973 of the Cavendish Laboratory of Experimental Physics where New Zealand's most famous scientist, Lord Rutherford of Nelson, was Director. It was here that he did the theoretical groundwork for harnessing atomic power. In 1973 the Cavendish was moved to Madingley Road in West Cambridge where it now stands; one of its buildings is called the Rutherford Building. Small groups are welcome to visit the museum of the Cavendish Laboratory at its new site by prior arrangement. Tel: (01223) 337-351.

A left turn at the end of Free School Lane will take the visitor up Downing Street at the end of which is Emmanuel, another college with links to early New

Zealand. William Rolleston (1831-1903), the last Superintendent of Canterbury before the abolition of the provinces in 1877, read classics at Emmanuel before emigrating to New Zealand. He carried his love of the classics with him to the new land for, when he was a bullock driver on the Canterbury Plains, he used to address his beasts in Latin and Greek. His statue is in front of the Canterbury Museum. Rolleston Avenue in Christchurch, the town of Rolleston and Mount Rolleston in the Arthur's Pass National Park are named after him.

While Emmanuel educated the last Superintendent of Canterbury it was its next door neighbour in Saint Andrew's Street, Christ's College, where its first Superintendent, James Edward Fitzgerald, graduated in mathematics in 1842. This eloquent Irishman took part in university debates and it was here that he honed his debating skills which served him so well during his later political career in New Zealand. Fitzgerald was not only the first Superintendent of Canterbury but also the first Premier of New Zealand and founder of the Christchurch Press. Fitzgerald Avenue in Christchurch is named after him and so is the South Canterbury town of Geraldine for that was the clan name of the Fitzgerald family in Ireland. James Edward Fitzgerald is a familiar figure to the people of Christchurch by his bronze statue at the southern end of Rolleston Avenue where he is gazing down Cashel Street.

Fitzgerald, who was assistant secretary of the British Museum before emigrating to New Zealand, was reputedly the first settler to land when the *Charlotte Jane* arrived in Lyttelton Harbour on 16th December, 1850. There were several men who were pushing to the front of the lifeboat in the hope of being the first Canterbury colonist ashore and Fitzgerald was behind them. However, when the moment came the big, burly and quick witted Fitzgerald leapfrogged over the backs of those who were ducking down in front of him and so became the first settler to set foot in Canterbury.

Across the road from Christ's College in Saint Andrew's Street is the church of Saint Andrew the Great. This is of special significance to New Zealanders for, buried under the central aisle, are Captain Cook's wife, Elizabeth, his son and namesake, James Cook, and another son, Hugh. Their names are engraved on the floor slabs above the graves while high up on the wall to the left of the altar is an impressive marble monument to the discoverer of New Zealand and his whole family. This was erected at his wife's request and the various inscriptions on the monument tell the bare facts of a particularly tragic story.

Neither Captain Cook nor his wife ever lived at Cambridge (See: East End of London, and Whitby, Yorkshire) but it seems that Mrs. Cook, who survived her husband by fifty-six years, wanted to make this the last resting place of the family. Cambridge was not an inappropriate choice since her husband, although the son of a farm labourer with very little formal education, had a first class scientific mind and in 1776 he was elected a member of the prestigious Royal Society which was dedicated to the advancement of science.

Some years after Captain Cook's death his youngest son, Hugh, a tall, fine youth, came up to Christ's College, across the road from this church, to study for the ministry. However, a few weeks after arriving in Cambridge he succumbed to a fever and died and was the first of his family to be buried here at Saint Andrew's. In support of this little church and its monument to her family Mrs. Elizabeth Cook gave £1,000 – a huge sum for those times.

And so to the story of the monument and its inscriptions, the first being "To the memory of Captain James Cook of the Royal Navy, one of the most celebrated Navigators that this, or former Ages can boast of: who was killed by the Natives of Owybee in the Pacific Ocean on the 14th day of February, 1779, in the 51st year of his Age" (Owybee was the old name for Hawaii).

After Captain Cook was speared in the back by a Hawaiian his body was hacked to pieces by the frenzied natives and the pieces were then distributed throughout the island. The crew managed to recover some of the body parts (the severed hands, the bones of the limbs and part of the skull) which were then placed in a coffin. On 21st February, a week after his death, the coffin was lowered into the blue waters of Kaawaloa Bay in the Pacific, the ocean that he had charted.

In the year following her husband's gory death Mrs. Cook lost her second son, who was a midshipman in the Navy. "And in memory of Nathaniel Cook, who was lost with the *Thunderer* man-of-war….in a most dreadful hurricane in October, 1780, aged 16 years".

IN MEMORY

of *CAPTAIN* JAMES COOK, of the ROYAL NAVY, one of the moſt celebrated Navigators, that this, or former Ages can boaſt of; who was killed by the Natives of *Owyhee*, in the *Pacific Ocean*, on the 14th Day of February, 1779; in the 51ſt Year of his Age.

Of Mr. NATHANIEL COOK, who was loſt with the *Thunderer* Man of War, Captain *Boyle Walſingham*, in a moſt dreadful Hurricane, in October, 1780; aged 16 Years.

Of Mr. HUGH COOK, of *Chriſt's College*, CAMBRIDGE, who died on the 21ſt of December, 1793; aged 17 Years.

Of JAMES COOK, Eſq; COMMANDER in the ROYAL NAVY, who loſt his Life on the 25th of January, 1794; in going from *Pool*, to the *Spitfire* Sloop of War, which he commanded; in the 31ſt Year of his Age.

Of ELIZ.th COOK, who died April 9th 1771, Aged 4 Years. JOSEPH COOK, who died Septr 13th 1768, Aged 1 Month GEORGE COOK, who died Octr 1^{ſt} 1772, Aged 4 Months.

All Children of the first mentioned CAP.^{t} JAMES COOK by ELIZABETH COOK, who survived her Husband 56 Years, & departed this life 13th May 1835, at her residence Clapham Surrey in the 94th Year of her Age. Her remains are deposited with those of her Sons JAMES & HUGH, in the middle Aisle of this Church.

Church of St. Andrew-the-Great, Cambridge
Photograph: John Bate-Williams
Memorial to Captain Cook and his family telling a particularly sad story. There is a remembrance service here on the Sunday closest to Anzac Day.

The *Thunderer* was lost off the coast of Jamaica and Nathaniel's body was never found.

Twelve years later Mrs. Cook was to lose her two surviving sons within five weeks of each other. "And in memory of Mr. Hugh Cook of Christ's College, Cambridge, who died on the 21st December, 1793, aged 17 years".

The next sentence is in memory of "James Cook, Esq., commander in the Royal Navy who lost his life on the 25th January, 1794, in going from Pool, to the *Spitfire* Sloop of War, which he commanded in the 31st year of his Age". His body was washed up on the Isle of Wight, unlike those of his naval father and brother, and is buried here at Saint Andrew's.

The memorial also honours the three Cook children who died in infancy, Elizabeth, Joseph and George.

After the death of the last of her six children Mrs. Cook lived for another forty-two years. She "departed this life 15th May, 1835, at her residence at Clapham, Surrey, in the 94th year of her Age".

On the monument is a mourning figure and there are naval objects at the top. Beneath the inscription is the coat-of-arms that was granted to the Cook family in 1785. On the shield are to be found two polar stars, top and bottom, and between them a map of the Pacific with every tenth degree of latitude marked and every fifteenth degree of longitude, the voyages of Captain Cook being traced in red. And the Motto? *Nil intentatum reliquit* (He leaves nothing untried). It was rare for a commoner to be granted a coat-of-arms and it shows the high esteem in which Cook was held by George III.

If the doors of Saint Andrew the Great are closed, entry can be gained by ringing one of the bells at the entrance. (Tel: 01223-518218) There is a special Anzac Day service in this church every year on the afternoon of the Sunday closest to 25th April when the flags of New Zealand and Australia are unfurled, both with the stars of the Southern Cross, which guided Cook south, and the Union Jack in the top left hand corner – a living and continuing link with the great sea captain who first raised the Union flag on our shores, thereby establishing that both countries would be members of the English speaking world.

The Anzac service is attended by representatives of the Australian and New Zealand High Commissions, the local Member of Parliament, the Lord Lieutenant of Cambridgeshire and members of the public. A Lord Lieutenant is the Queen's personal representative in a shire.

Two miles east of Cambridge on the Newmarket Road is the Cambridge City Cemetery, which is opposite the airport. In the Air Forces Plot are the graves of eighty-one New Zealand airmen who were killed on operations over the United Kingdom. Most of them were from Bomber Command bases in Lincolnshire and Fighter stations in Norfolk and Suffolk. The nearest station is at Barnwell, half a mile away.

The Air Forces Plot is bordered by a yew hedge and in spring the daffodils flower around the headstones. There is a shelter that has two oak seats and a bronze box containing the Register of the names of the dead. A perfect place to sit and absorb the tranquillity and beauty of the surroundings and to reflect on the supreme sacrifice that was made by the young airmen of the 1940s so that the rest of us could live in peace and relative freedom.

Cambridge can be reached by train from London's Liverpool Street station. The journey is approximately an hour and a half.

HUNTINGDONSHIRE

Kimbolton

The small farming town of Kimbolton in the Rangitikei was named after the country seat of the Dukes of Manchester, the seventh duke being the chairman of the Emigrants' and Colonists' Aid Corporation which in 1871 sponsored the purchase of the huge Manchester block south of Kimbolton between the Manawatu and Rangitikei rivers.

The town of Kimbolton, midway between Cambridge and Northampton on the B645, has a wide main street with colourful period houses that retain something of the atmosphere of the place when Katherine of Aragon, the first of Henry VIII's six wives, lived here after she ceased to be Queen.

NORTHAMPTONSHIRE

Naseby

The village of Naseby, just off the A14 ten miles west of Kettering, was the scene of a famous battle in 1645 in which Oliver Cromwell's Puritan army defeated the royal forces of Charles I and his faithful lieutenant, Prince Rupert.

The Otago town of Naseby is named after Naseby in Northamptonshire while the town of Cromwell in Otago, less than fifty miles as the crow flies from Naseby, is named after the Puritan victor of the battle.

LEICESTERSHIRE

Little Bowden

In the south of this famous hunting shire is Little Bowden, to-day part of the town of Market Handborough (off the A6 south-east of Leicester) but in the nineteenth century a rural hamlet where life went on much as it had for generations. It was here that Kathleen Nunneley, the pioneer champion of New Zealand women's tennis, was born in 1872.

When she emigrated to New Zealand at the age of twenty-one she had already played in quite a few tournaments in England. In the new land she was in a class of her own, winning 13 successive national singles titles from 1895 to 1907, more than any other person in the history of New Zealand tennis. She also won 10 women's doubles titles and 9 mixed doubles, on two occasions of which she partnered Anthony Wilding.

In 1928 she had all the gold medals that she had won made into a trophy, the Nunneley Casket, which is the cup for inter-provincial women's tennis. In short, New Zealand tennis owes a lot to the lady from Little Bowden.

OXFORDSHIRE

Oxford

"Yet, O ye spires of Oxford! Domes and towers!
Gardens and groves! Your presence overpowers."

- William Wordsworth

Like Cambridge, the university city of Oxford has numerous links with New Zealand - especially with the founding of Canterbury. Indeed, the city of Christchurch is named after Christ Church College, Oxford, because several of the members of the Canterbury Association were educated there, including its leader, John Robert Godley, who studied Classics. When the first four ships sailed to Lyttelton in 1850 to found the Canterbury settlement they carried on board a reference library of some two thousand books which were the gift of Christ Church College, Oxford, which can fairly be regarded as the fount of learning for Canterbury, if not for New Zealand.

Christ Church College, Oxford
The largest city in the South Island was named after this college where Godley and other founders of Canterbury were educated. The college donated 2,000 books to form a reference library for the new settlement on the Canterbury Plains. These books came on the First Four Ships and were the fount of learning in New Zealand.

Christ Church, overlooking Christ Church Meadow at the southern end of the town, is the largest Oxford college and is the only one to have a cathedral as its chapel. Among its alumni was John Wesley, the founder of Methodism. Between 1855 and 1881 it had a mathematics lecturer called Charles Lutwidge Dodgson who is better known as Lewis Carroll, the author of *Alice in Wonderland*.

In view of this early historical link between Christ Church College and the founding of Canterbury it was particularly appropriate that this should be the college that educated both Joseph Banks, after whom Canterbury's Banks Peninsula is named, and George Ranald MacDonald (1892-1967) who compiled the Dictionary of Canterbury Biography – a series of cards in the Canterbury Museum recording the careers and families of 12,000 Canterbury people.

From Christ Church cathedral a short walk across Merton Field takes you to Merton College. Several New Zealanders have studied here including former All Black, Chris Laidlaw, and the poet, novelist and soldier, John Mulgan (1911-45), who wrote the New Zealand classic *Man Alone*. The son of distinguished writer, Alan Mulgan, John took a first class in English Honours here at Merton. On the outbreak of war in 1939 he enlisted in the army and was killed in its last hours, news of his death reaching his wife and young son in Wellington on VE Day. Shades of that other soldier-poet, Wilfred Owen, news of whose death in the First World War reached London after the Armistice.

Only a short walk from Merton through the Botanic Gardens is Magdalen College which is where Arthur Porritt arrived in 1923 as a Rhodes Scholar. He later became the first New Zealand born Governor-General (1967-72). For three years Porritt represented Oxford University at athletics and in 1924 he won the bronze medal in the 100 metre sprint at the Olympic Games in Paris.

Porritt was the captain of the New Zealand Olympic team at both Paris and Amsterdam (1928) and was the team manager at the Berlin Olympics in 1936. He was later Surgeon to the Queen. His son, Jonathan, also studied at Magdalen before moving on to become a leader of the environmental movement in Britain.

Proceeding along High Street from Magdalen the first college on the left is University College which is where Lord Bledisloe, Governor-General from 1929 to 1934, studied law. He later became a Fellow of the College. This popular Governor donated the Bledisloe Cup for rugby matches between the All Blacks and the Wallabies. (See: Inns of Court and City of London)

The next college on the same side of High Street is Oriel which is where Cecil Rhodes received his university education. So wonderful did he consider his Oxford experience that under his generous will he established the famous Rhodes scholarships which every year enable two New Zealand students to do their post-graduate studies at Oxford. Rhodes wisely did not confine the scholarships to "swots"; there are three criteria – sound academic achievement, good character and proficiency in manly outdoor sports – which explains why athletes like Arthur Porritt and Jack Lovelock and All Blacks like David Kirk and Chris Laidlaw have been able to add an Oxford education to their sporting feats.

On the other side of High Street is Brasenose College which also has a number of connections with New Zealand and with Canterbury in particular. Sir John Cracroft Wilson, an early runholder in Canterbury, entered Brasenose as a student in 1826. Wilson served in India and when he arrived at Lyttelton in 1854 he brought with him a retinue of Indian servants. He bought a block of land at the foot of the hills which he named Cashmere after the Himalayan area of India which to-day is known as the troubled province of Kashmir (an alternative spelling of Cashmere).

Another Canterbury runholder, Sir Robert Heaton Rhodes (1861-1956), took his M.A. at Brasenose (See: Saint Paul's Cathedral, London). A member of one of New Zealand's grandest families, Rhodes possessed all the finest qualities of the gentry. Generous and patriotic, he served as Minister of Defence from 1920 to 1926, in which capacity he was instrumental in acquiring Wigram air base in Christchurch and establishing the air force. Unlike the greedy politicians of to-day, Rhodes entered politics out of a sense of *noblesse oblige*. Another product of Brasenose was John Middleton Murry, the husband of Katherine Mansfield.

Brasenose was where William Webb Ellis came to further his studies after leaving Rugby School where, legend has it, he picked up the ball and ran with it, thereby establishing a new sport which was to make an important contribution to the future character of distant lands like New Zealand and South Africa.

It is interesting to note that the two most important cups for which the All Blacks play, the Webb Ellis Cup, which is the official name for the World Cup, and the Bledisloe Cup for matches against Australia, are both named in honour of men who were educated here at Oxford at colleges only a few yards away from each other.

Turning right off High Street at All Saints church one passes Lincoln College on the right and then Exeter College. It was here that another New Zealand Rhodes Scholar, Jack Lovelock, arrived in 1931. Lovelock was elected President of the Oxford University Athletic Club. He is best remembered for his win in the 1,500 metres at the Berlin Olympics in 1936 when he broke the world record. He thus became the first New Zealander to win a gold medal in athletics at the Olympic Games.

Behind Exeter College is the Sheldonian Theatre where the degree ceremonies take place. It was here, on the anniversary of Agincourt in 1945, that six of the leaders of the Second World War were each given an honorary Doctorate of Civil Law. Those so honoured were General Eisenhower, Montgomery of Alamein, Field-Marshal Alan Brooke, General Tovey, Air Chief Marshal Tedder and General Freyberg, the commander of the New Zealand Division. The Public Orator of Oxford, Mr. Higham, declared to the assembled guests that Freyberg had as many distinctions as the wounds he had received in battle.

Passing along Broad Street from Exeter College one reaches the church of Saint Mary Magdalene at the southern end of the street known as Saint Giles. The second college on the right of Saint Giles is Trinity which is where Sir George Bowen, Governor of New Zealand from 1868 to 1873, took his B.A. degree with first class Honours in Classics. Bowen Street, alongside Parliament in Wellington, is named after him.

Across Saint Giles from Trinity is Beaumont Street which leads to Worcester College where former All Black captain, David Kirk, did his post-graduate studies. Another product of Worcester was Bishop Churchill Julius, the second bishop of Christchurch, who took his M.A. here in 1873.

Returning to Saint Giles and continuing in a northerly direction, take the left fork into Woodstock Road and Somerville College is on the left. It was founded as a college for women students and Kiri Te Kanawa, who in 1983 was awarded an honorary doctorate of Music by Oxford University, is one of its Fellows.

Like its sister university city of Cambridge, Oxford is the resting place of New Zealand servicemen. A mile and a half west of the city of Oxford is the Oxford (Botley) Cemetery. It is on the south side of the A420 between Oxford and Botley, just east of the junction with the A34. It is situated in North Hinskey Lane.

The war graves plot is south of the chapel and is easily recognised by the Cross of Sacrifice in the centre. Buried here are sixty-three New Zealand servicemen – nine from the First World War and the rest from the 1939-45 War. The latter were air crew, serving at nearby bases.

Abingdon

The town of Abingdon, ten miles south of Oxford and just over the border in Berkshire, is a "sister-town" of Thames in New Zealand.

This special relationship developed out of the Second World War when, in the face of rationing and the sinking by German U-boats of convoys carrying food to Britain, a "More Food to Britain" committee was formed in New Zealand to send food parcels to the beleaguered people in the Mother Country.

The people of Thames, New Zealand, chose Abingdon-on-Thames because it was comparable in size to their own town and was situated on the River Thames; until rationing ended in Britain in 1952, a lot of food parcels were sent from Thames to Abingdon where they were gratefully received by the townsfolk.

As a mark of appreciation the then borough council of Abingdon presented an illuminated "Address of Thanks" to Thames, New Zealand. Then in 1966 the Honorary Freedom of Abingdon was conferred on the Mayor and councillors of Thames. This was only the seventh time in more than four centuries that Abingdon had conferred its Honorary Freedom and the first time that it had been granted overseas.

In proposing the resolution Alderman James Candy recalled receiving one of the food parcels, "There was sugar, butter, cheese, dried fruit, milo, eggs and a tiny Christmas pudding." All pretty run of the mill stuff to us but to people suffering ever shorter rations, not to mention the risk of being bombed, the receipt of a food parcel from New Zealand must have seemed like manna from Heaven.

Seconding the motion Alderman Liversidge said, "The people of Thames are, by origin, our kinsmen, but they are much more, they are our staunchest friends."

In explaining the resolution Alderman J. Stanley added, "It (the granting of the Honorary Freedom) is the only way that a town can say thank-you to those who do not wish to be thanked."

The relationship was given a further dimension in September, 1972, when the Thames Borough Council sent to Abingdon twenty native trees, including pohutukawa, in recognition of the close ties between these two towns at the opposite ends of the earth.

A photograph of the Abingdon Town Hall can be seen in the council offices at Thames while on a staircase landing in the Council Chamber in the Guildhall at Abingdon is a large coloured aerial photograph of Thames that was taken by Whites Aviation.

Abingdon's history began with the founding of an Abbey on the site in 675 A.D. In East Saint Helen's

Street can be seen houses dating from 1550 that are still being lived in. There is an ancient custom that on special occasions councillors gather on the flat roof of the historic County Hall (now part of Abingdon Museum) and throw buns down to the people in the square below.

Little Coxwell

Several miles west of Abingdon and just off the A420 is the village of Little Coxwell. In its church is a memorial window to Rev. Vicesimus Lush who was a curate here before emigrating to New Zealand with his wife, four children and fifteen year old maid, Betsy. In New Zealand Rev. Lush served as a pioneer vicar at both Howick, Auckland, and Saint George's church at Thames. He was the first resident vicar at Howick where he lived in Ewelme Cottage, which is one of the few pioneer houses in Auckland to have been preserved. It was owned by the Lush family for 105 years before being opened to the public.

Blenheim Palace

The capital of the province of Marlborough in the South Island shares its name with one of the greatest palaces in Europe here in rural Oxfordshire. Both, of course, are named after the Battle of Blenheim in 1704 in which a great victory over the French was won by John Churchill, the first Duke of Marlborough and the ancestor of Sir Winston Churchill. As a result of this battle the names "Blenheim" and "Marlborough" have ever since been inextricably linked – no less in New Zealand than elsewhere.

Blenheim Palace, four miles north-west of Oxford on the A44, is one of the finest examples of Baroque architecture in England. It was built by a grateful nation and presented to the first Duke of Marlborough. It is set in 2,100 acres of parkland which includes Water Terraces, an Italian Garden, Rose Garden and Arboretum.

Inside the palace the visitor can see the simple room in which Sir Winston Churchill was born prematurely on 30th November, 1874.

Blenheim Palace is open daily (10.30 a.m. to 5.30 p.m.) from mid March to the end of October while the park is open every day from 9 to 4.45 p.m.

On the south side of Blenheim Park is the little village of Bladon where Sir Winston Churchill is buried in the churchyard.

Shipton-under-Wychwood

This exotically named village is on the A361 south of Chipping Norton. On its village green is a Gothic style obelisk in memory of seventeen people from just two local families who sailed off to a new life in New Zealand on board the 1,200 ton vessel, *Cospatrick*. She left Gravesend on 11th September, 1874, with 433 passengers but caught on fire about three hundred miles south-west of the Cape of Good Hope with almost total loss of life.

WARWICKSHIRE

Birmingham

In the south-west of Birmingham on the A38 is Selly Oak, the site of the Birmingham (Lodge Hill) Cemetery which contains the graves of nine New Zealand servicemen – eight from the First World War and one from the Second.

The First World War plot is in the southern part of the cemetery and the graves are marked by stones set in the grass in the manner of a lawn cemetery. On three sides are screen walls that bear the names of those who are buried here. The Second World War plot is in the eastern part of the cemetery.

Coventry

During the Second World War the city of Coventry was all but wiped out in only a few hours; on the night of 14th November, 1940, some three hundred German bombers carried out a massive attack in which 507 civilians were killed and most of the central city was burned by incendiary bombs. It was during this raid that Coventry Cathedral was almost totally destroyed, with only its strong outer wall left standing. While the fires were still smouldering two of the charred lengths of timber were formed into a cross and placed above a temporary altar. From this point and with this inspiration a new cathedral rose alongside the old one.

The charred cross still stands among the ruins of the old building. To-day the juxtaposition of the two cathedrals sharing a common wall, the one a bombed ruin and the other, like the Resurrection, a renewed House of God, is a symbol of old and new, of war and peace.

The new cathedral is made of greyish-pink sandstone that was quarried in the neighbouring county of Staffordshire. It was designed by the noted British architect, Sir Basil Spence. However, not all of Spence's buildings are as beautiful as Coventry's cathedral; he also designed the Beehive at Parliament Buildings, Wellington.

The best way to enter the cathedral is from the ruins of the old, through the Queen's Arch, one of the arches of the old cathedral so-called because Her Majesty laid the foundation stone of the new cathedral under this arch in 1956.

From the arch the Queen's Steps lead down to the west door of the cathedral. From the top of the steps one can see through the glass of the west wall all the way down the nave to the great tapestry, the largest in the world, above the altar.

The purpose of this seventy foot high glass wall is to merge the old and the new cathedrals into a unified whole. On its ninety-six panels of clear glass are etched figures of angels and saints. This magnificent feature was designed and executed by the talented New Zealand glass artist, John Hutton. After leaving Wanganui Collegiate Hutton became a lawyer and practised for several years. After his marriage his wife convinced him to develop his artistic talents and they moved to England.

The intention of his work at Coventry was to show that it is through history and suffering that one gains a perspective of the present and the future. Thus the top row of his masterpiece depicts patriarchs and prophets from the Old Testamant while the second row shows figures from the New Testament. In the third row are some English saints while the bottom row features saints who have a special association with this part of the Midlands and the old kingdom of Mercia.

Coventry Cathedral is one of the most beautiful buildings of the modern world and Hutton's glass wall is the jewel in its crown. Over the years New Zealand has relied heavily on Britain for its architecture and works of art; treasures like Hutton's wall at Coventry and the stage hangings that the Wellington Shakespeare Society made for the Globe Theatre are the return gifts.

John Hutton also created the fine etched glass at the entrance of Wellington's Saint Paul's Cathedral. His ashes are interred at the foot of his great wall of glass here at Coventry.

This is not the only link between these two post-war cathedrals, Coventry and Wellington, for they also happen to be the only two cathedrals in the world that lie in a north/south position instead of the usual east/west which had its origins in the practice of facing European cathedrals towards Bethlehem – a practice that has been carried on in the Antipodes despite the different geographical position.

Saint Paul's Cathedral in Wellington is also a member of the "Coventry Cross" family of cathedrals which are dedicated to reconciliation between peoples. This means that it has a "Coventry Cross" – a simple cross made of three nails that were salvaged from the bombed ruin of Coventry Cathedral. They have been silvered over to form a "Coventry Cross" and in Wellington it is mounted on the Dean's desk in the Nave.

In Windsor Street, Coventry, are Wellington Gardens, which are homes for elderly people. Built after the Second World War, they are named after New Zealand's capital city. The story is as follows.

In the autumn of 1940 Hitler switched his attacks from England's airfields to its crowded cities in a futile attempt to break the morale of the people. The Fuhrer never did understand that, while he could walk over all the nations of the Continent, the British, unconquered since 1066, were made of different stuff. However, his onslaught against the civilian population did lead to thousands of them being bombed out of their homes by the Luftwaffe.

The Lord Mayor of London set up an Air-Raid Distress Fund for the purpose of helping old people who had been made homeless by the bombing. In 1940-1 the loyal and generous people of Wellington donated £60,000 to the fund and the Lord Mayor passed on half of it to Coventry where it was used to build Wellington Gardens.

The bombing of Coventry and its cathedral and their re-birth from the ashes is one of the great stories of modern times – a tale of suffering, hope, courage, forgiveness and tremendous imagination. Before that terrible night, when Hitler sent his bombers on their mission of destruction, Coventry was just another industrial city of the Midlands. To-day its cathedral stands with Westminster Abbey and Saint Paul's, Canterbury and York, as one of the most fascinating and most visited places in Britain. To visit Coventry and see with one's own eyes what has been achieved is indeed an uplifting and enriching experience.

Rugby

The famous Rugby School in the town of that name in Warwickshire was founded in 1567. It was here in 1823 that the game of rugby originated when William Webb Ellis is said to have picked up the ball in his hands and run forward with it during a kicking game that was the forerunner of modern soccer. It is important to remember that this was only the first step in an evolutionary process that culminated in rugby as we know it to-day.

At this time there was no uniformity in ball kicking games and each school seemed to develop its own type of football. Because of the presence of paving stones on the playground Charterhouse and Winchester schools developed a dribbling game which was to become soccer while the vast green expanse at Rugby made for bodily contact and mauling. Mauls, in fact, were the main feature of the early game with domination by the forwards and a rather leisurely game

Rugby - Photograph: John Bate-Williams
Statue of William Webb Ellis, the legendary founder of the game of rugby, after whom the World Cup is named. Situated near the entrance to Rugby School.

for the backs. The whole aim was for a team to push itself over the opponents' goal line so as to be awarded a try.

William Webb Ellis' effort took place in the Close at Rugby School, which is little changed to-day. In the grounds of the school can be seen a plaque bearing the words: "This stone commemorates the exploit of William Webb Ellis who, with a fine disregard for the rules of football as played in his time, first took the ball in his arms and ran with it thus originating the distinctive feature of the rugby game. A.D. 1823". Webb Ellis left Rugby in 1825 and went up to Oxford before becoming an Anglican priest. His name is remembered in the World Cup, which is officially called "The Webb Ellis Cup", and there is a statue of him just around the corner from Rugby School in Dunchurch Road.

The rugby balls at that time were made out of pigs' bladders that were inserted into hand stitched leather casings. The bladder of each swine would be blown up while still in a fairly raw (and smelly!) state. This was done by lung power down the stem of a clay pipe that was inserted into the opening of the bladder.

The firm of Gilbert's, which made boots and shoes for the boys at the school, also made the footballs in this way; rugby enthusiasts to-day can visit the James Gilbert Rugby Museum which is housed in a building where the Gilberts have been making rugby balls since 1842. To-day their balls, produced here in Rugby, are used in Test matches throughout the world.

The museum is full of rugby mementos and the visitor can watch the balls being hand made. The Gilbert Museum, situated at 5 Saint Matthew's Street, Rugby, is open Monday – Friday from 9 to 5.30 p.m. and on Saturdays from 9 to 5. Admission is free and there is a wide range of souvenirs on sale.

There is also a Museum of Rugby School which is across the road from the school at 10 Little Church Street. It tells the story of Rugby School and its famous game. Old boys (Rugbeians) include Sir James Fergusson, Governor of New Zealand from June, 1873, to December, 1874, and the grandfather of Sir Bernard Fergusson, Lewis Carroll, the author of *Alice In Wonderland*, Neville Chamberlain, British Prime Minister at the beginning of the Second World War, the soldier-poet, Rupert Brooke, who died on the way to Gallipoli, and William Gisborne (1825-98) who was Minister of Public Works in New Zealand in 1870 and 1871 and after whom the East Coast city of Gisborne is named (See: Derby). The Museum and its gift shop are open Monday-Saturday from 10.30 to 12.30 and 1.30 to 4.30 with guided tours leaving from there each day at 2 p.m.

At the Home of Rugby Football Visitor Centre, 4 Lawrence Sheriff Street, Rugby, there is a presentation of the town and its famous people by ex-Welsh rugby player, Cliff Morgan.

Rupert Brooke's statue can be seen in the Jubilee Gardens in Regent Street, Rugby. During his short and memorable life Brooke managed to sail as far as New Zealand for a visit. When he joined the Royal

Naval Division on the outbreak of the First World War his company commander was Bernard Freyberg, the future Governor-General. They shared a cabin on the *Grantully Castle*, which took them from Avonmouth, near Bristol, to Gallipoli. Alas, poor Rupert died forty-eight hours before the landings and was buried in an olive grove on the Greek island of Skyros, Freyberg being one of the burial party. A few hours later Freyberg did his famous swim to light the flares on the beaches to distract the Turks from where the real landings were to take place.

Of particular interest to the visitor is the Rugby Pathway of Fame, which was installed for the Rugby World Cup in 1999 when many fans from all over the world came as pilgrims to this fount of their favourite game. The Pathway consists of a two mile walk around the town and there is a series of forty-seven commemorative plaques that record landmarks of both the town and the game. The first of these plaques was unveiled during the 1999 World Cup by ex-Springbok, Naas Botha.

The town of Rugby is as far inland as it is possible to go in Britain – rather like Taupo in the North Island. It is an hour by train from London.

Stratford-upon-Avon

This beautiful town on the Avon, the birthplace of the greatest writer in the English language, was the inspiration for the town of Stratford at the foot of Mount Egmont. The streets in the New Zealand town of

Stratford are named after famous characters in Shakespeare's plays and the town hosts a Shakespeare Festival every two years. Furthermore, its clock tower has recently been rebuilt in the mock Tudor style redolent of the times in which Shakespeare lived.

There are no direct descendants of William Shakespeare as his line died out on the death of his granddaughter, Elizabeth, without issue. However, there are still some descendants of Shakespeare's sister, Joan, who married William Hart. Two of their descendants, the sisters Ellen and Mary Hart, married two brothers from nearby Evesham, John and William Ashley, in the 1840s. Children of both these marriages emigrated to New Zealand where they settled in the Invercargill area; some of their descendants still live in the South Island although none now bear the surname of Hart.

WORCESTERSHIRE

"Hawkes Bay, more than any other province in New Zealand, reminds me of my native Worcestershire. Not indeed the northern part of the county over which the sulphurous haze of the Black Country still hangs and thickens the sky, but the south where the pastures are lush and full of clover and the water-meadows which line the banks of Avon slope gently upward to the plum and apple orchards of the Evesham Vale."

Lord Cobham, Governor-General 1957-62, during a speech at Napier to mark the Hawke's Bay centenary on 1st November, 1958.

Hagley

Hagley Hall, in Worcestershire, twelve miles south-west of Birmingham on the A456, is one of the last of the great Palladian houses in England. It has been the home of the Lyttelton family (the Viscounts Cobham) since it was completed in 1760 at a time when nearby Birmingham was still a small village.

When the Canterbury Association was short of funds before the arrival of the first four ships, Lord George Lyttelton (1817-76), the Association's chairman, and some others advanced some tens of thousands of pounds of their own money to save the project from disaster. This was done out of respect for John Robert Godley, who was organising the new settlement, and as a mark of their faith in the venture.

In appreciation of this selfless gesture the Company named the port in Canterbury where they landed "Lyttelton" while a four hundred acre wilderness of fern, flax, toe toe and low scrub was set aside in the proposed city of Christchurch and named Hagley Park after Lord Lyttelton's family seat here in Worcestershire. Lord Lyttelton himself visited Canterbury in 1868 to see what had become of the venture in which he showed so much faith. He can not have been disappointed as by then Hagley Park had been converted into fine parkland and colourful gardens.

The Lyttelton family's association with New Zealand was continued with the appointment of his great-grandson, Viscount Cobham, as Governor-General in 1957. With eight young children he and his wife set a fine example of family life and carried out the role of Queen's representative in New Zealand with great style and dignity. At the end of his term of office some of his magnificent speeches were published in book form and sold thousands of copies. Both the Cobham Oval in Whangarei and the Cobham Outward Bound School in the Marlborough Sounds are named in honour of this popular and sporting Governor who in his younger days was vice-captain of the M.C.C.

The present Viscount Cobham, who was educated at Christ's College, Christchurch, during his family's time in New Zealand, inherited Hagley Hall and its 2,000 acres in 1977 on the death of his father. He is married to Doctor Lisa Clayton, the first woman to sail single-handedly and non-stop around the world.

It is possible to visit this historic home and see the wonderful Rococo plasterwork by Francesco Vassali as well as paintings by van Dyck, Reynolds and Lely. There are also portraits of Lord George Lyttelton and Viscount Cobham, the late Governor-General. Teas can be had in the house.

Hagley Hall is just off the Birmingham-Kidderminster Road, twelve miles from Birmingham. The nearest station is Hagley, which is one mile from the Hall. It is open normal hours in the summer but less regularly in winter. For details: Tel. (01562) 882408

Kidderminster

Four miles south-west of Hagley Hall on the A456 is the town of Kidderminster which is famous for its carpets. It was here that Walter Nash was born on 12th February, 1882, in a small, two storeyed brick cottage at 93 Mill Street. Nash was Prime Minister of New Zealand at the time that Lord Cobham was Governor-General and so New Zealand's two chief office holders hailed from this tiny corner of rural Worcestershire.

Nash was born into a poor family and his father was an alcoholic. He attended Saint John's School in Chapel Street, Kidderminster. The family then moved to Selly Oak on the outskirts of Birmingham where young Walter worked as a clerk in a bicycle factory for twelve years. It was in Selly Oak that he married Lotty Eaton and set up two shops – one selling tobacco and the other confectionery.

It might be thought strange that this man, whose 1957-60 Labour Government brought in the "Black Budget" which increased the duty on tobacco by a huge amount, should have been a tobacconist. Of course, by the time of the Black Budget, Nash no longer had any interests in tobacco since politicians go to a lot of trouble to protect from taxation those industries in which their own money is invested.

Nash, who spent much of his three year term as Prime Minister travelling abroad, returned to Kidderminster on several occasions and was made a Freeman of the Town.

SHROPSHIRE

Boscobel House and the Royal Oak

Ten miles east of Telford is Boscobel House, a seventeenth century hunting lodge where Charles II took refuge after his defeat in the Battle of Worcester in 1651. When Cromwell's troops came in search of him the wily king ran out to the garden and hid in an oak tree. This became famous among his supporters as the Royal Oak. A descendant of this historic tree can still be seen on the spot where the original stood.

Some of the acorns from the original tree were collected by George Graham who took them to New Zealand when he was secretary to Governor Hobson in 1840. He planted some of them in the grounds of Government House, Auckland, and others at a spot south of the township where they quickly grew into a large grove of trees which became known as Royal Oak.

In the warmer climate of Auckland the oaks grew much faster than in England but they also matured earlier and often decayed with the result that the trees planted by Mr. Graham no longer exist although the district where they were planted still bears the historic Stuart name of Royal Oak.

After Cromwell's soldiers left, Charles came out of the oak tree and spent the night inside Boscobel House. The tiny hiding place where he slept can still be seen. Boscobel House is open daily (except Mondays in winter) from 10 a.m. to 6 p.m. (4 p.m. in winter). It is situated a mile north of the M54 (Junction 3).

HEREFORDSHIRE

Hereford

Hereford, the cathedral city in the land of cider, is where Anthony Wilding's family came from. Frederick Wilding, the father of New Zealand's greatest tennis player, was educated at Hereford Cathedral School. He was also one of Herefordshire's best all-round athletes.

Anthony Wilding's maternal grandfather, Mr. Anthony (after whom he was named) was Mayor of Hereford and the Wilding home in Christchurch, New Zealand, was named "Fownhope" after the lovely village of Fownhope, a few miles south-east of Hereford. In the dining room of the Green Man Inn at Fownhope is a mural of the village's most famous son, Thomas Winter who, under the name "Tom Spring", was the boxing champion of England in the golden age of pugilism in the years after Waterloo. His family, like the Wildings, later settled in Christchurch. The author is one of his descendants.

While Anthony Wilding was a law student at Cambridge he found time between his studies and his tennis to play first class county cricket for Herefordshire (as well as being a motor cycle champion). This was in the years before the narrowing impact of specialisation made such healthy, all-round achievement impossible.

STAFFORDSHIRE

Lichfield

"Ah, lovely Lichfield! That so long hast shone
In blended charms, peculiarly thine own;
Stately, yet rural; through thy choral day,
Though shady, cheerful, and though quiet, gay."

- Anna Seward, *The Anniversary*, 1769

A few miles north of Birmingham is Lichfield with its fourteenth century cathedral that was built out of locally quarried Midland sandstone on the site of its predecessor. It is famous for its three graceful spires, known as "The Ladies of the Vale" and for its many treasures which include beautiful works of silver and embroidery as well as The Lichfield Gospels which date from the year 730. Written in Latin, they have been in the cathedral since the tenth century.

During the Civil War Lichfield suffered more than any other cathedral. It was attacked first by the Roundheads and later by the Royalists. Cannon balls that were fired against its walls can be seen in the cathedral's Visitors' Study Centre. Even tombs were desecrated by Cromwell's vandals.

George Augustus Selwyn, the first Bishop of New Zealand (1842-68), was the Bishop of Lichfield

Bishop Selwyn's tomb – Photograph: Lichfield Cathedral.

after he returned to England from his twenty-six years in New Zealand. During his tenure at Lichfield Selwyn, who had been responsible for building so many churches in New Zealand, extended the Bishop's Palace.

His marble effigy can be seen in the small Selwyn Chapel which is entered from the Lady Chapel on the south side. The tiled walls of the Selwyn Chapel depict aspects of his life in New Zealand. There is also a stained glass window showing water being brought to King David from the well at Bethlehem. It was commissioned by Bishop Selwyn to commemorate the brave act of an unknown Maori woman who, during the hostilities of 1864, stole out of Gate Pa near Tauranga at considerable risk from the firing to fetch water for the wounded British soldiers who were trapped inside the pa.

Bishop Selwyn's grave is at the east end of the burial ground outside the Lady Chapel. Buried nearby is Rev. Frederick Thatcher (1814-90) who trained as an architect before taking Holy Orders. In 1843 Thatcher emigrated to New Zealand and designed several churches including Old Saint Paul's in Wellington. Rev. Thatcher believed that Gothic – and preferably Decorated Gothic – was the only true style for Anglican churches. In New Zealand this Associate of the Royal Institute of British Architects had to translate his principles from the stone of England to the wood of New Zealand. He was Selwyn's secretary and followed the bishop when he moved from New Zealand to

Lichfield. There is a memorial to him in the north choir aisle of the cathedral.

This cathedral town gave its name to the small settlement of Lichfield in the Waikato. Its promoters had big ideas for their scheme of colonising Lichfield and the surrounding land and that is why they chose the name of this ancient cathedral town of England. Unfortunately, it never took off and Lichfield to-day is a small one-horse town just like thousands of others throughout New Zealand. But at least it has a grandiose name!

Cannock Chase

Travelling north-east on the M6 from Birmingham one comes to the area known as Cannock Chase, an expanse of fairly barren hills that are bounded by the town of Cannock in the west, Rugeley in the east and Stafford in the north.

During the First World War there were two huge army camps on Cannock Chase to train the soldiers before they were sent to the killing fields of France. The quarter million British and Commonwealth troops who were camped here included tens of thousands of New Zealanders.

Cannock Chase was a former royal hunting forest – hence its name. Later it was a source of fuel for the Tudor iron industry. On the outbreak of war in 1914 the owner of the Chase, Lord Lichfield, granted it to the army for two camps. To-day there is not much evidence of the 1,500 huts and other amenities that were home to all these soldiers.

In the Commonwealth War Cemetery at Broadhurst Green, south of Brocton (near the Telecom tower), are the graves of seventy-one New Zealand soldiers, mainly from the New Zealand Rifle Brigade which was based here. On the Sunday closest to Anzac Day there is a memorial service at the cemetery which, apart from Gallipoli, is believed to be the largest outside Australia and New Zealand with attendance figures usually exceeding 2,000. However, most of the New Zealanders who are buried here died not of battle wounds but of the terrible Spanish flu which swept the world at the end of 1918 and killed millions. Each headstone bears the personal details and regimental badge of the deceased.

To-day there are information centres at Milford and Marquis Drive which are open on Saturdays and Sundays from 2 p.m. until 5.30 p.m. Maps can be obtained there showing walking tracks around the sites of the old camps.

There is also the Museum of Cannock Chase in Valley Road, Hednesford, Cannock, which is open from Easter until the end of September every day from 11 to 5 and from October until Easter, Mon.- Fri. 11 to 4. Admission is free and there is space for twelve touring caravans throughout the year.

One of the more touching memorials can be found just south of the Coppice Hill car park, off Chase Road south of Brocton. It is a granite memorial that marks the resting place of "Freda".

Freda, a Dalmatian bitch, was the four legged mascot of the New Zealand Rifle Brigade and, when she died in 1918, they buried her here and put up a headstone in her memory. The masonry deteriorated over the years and was replaced by the present monument, which was dedicated in October, 2001, in the presence of about seventy people and their dogs. Freda's dog collar is on display at the Military Museum at Waiouru, New Zealand.

In addition to its links with the New Zealand Army Cannock Chase has many attractions for the nature lover. Its 3,500 acres include lowland heath, ancient woodland, working forest and a herd of approximately seven hundred fallow deer that roam freely throughout the Chase. There are several self-guided walks and cycling routes that start at the Marquis Drive Visitor Centre. Bicycles are available for hire. And the good news is that, unlike in New Zealand, the cyclist in Britain has the right to decide for himself whether or not to wear a helmet. It's called "freedom of choice".

Stafford

In May, 1919, the New Zealand troops from Cannock Chase paraded in Market Square, Stafford, and were presented with a Union Jack and a silk New Zealand ensign by the Mayor as a farewell gesture. A film of the ceremony was placed in a special casket and sent to the government in New Zealand.

Trentham

North Staffordshire is famous for its pleasure parks – Alton Towers and Trentham Gardens. The latter are in the grounds of Trentham Hall which is on the A34 north of Stafford and just south of Stoke-on-Trent. Trentham Hall was built in the early seventeenth century by an ancestor of the Duke of Sutherland. One of the titles of the Duke of Sutherland is Viscount Trentham and it was in honour of Viscount Trentham, who was created Duke of Sutherland in 1833, that the settlement at the top of the Hutt Valley, famous for its military camp and racecourse, was named.

The gardens here at Trentham, Staffs, cover some seven hundred acres and include a boating lake, swimming pool, miniature railway and a site for caravans and camping.

DERBYSHIRE

Derby

During the Jacobite rebellion of 1745 Bonnie Prince Charlie's army of kilted clansmen crossed the border into England in a daring but ultimately doomed attempt to restore the Stuarts to the Throne of England. The Scotsmen got as far as Derby which was a three day march from London. However, the generals – but not the Prince himself – lost their nerve here in Derby and decided to retreat back to Scotland. This was the beginning of the end for the Stuart cause – an end that was played out in the bloodbath of Culloden four months later.

To commemorate these stirring days the city fathers commissioned a bronze equestrian statue of the Prince which stands behind the cathedral on the green by the Old Silk Mill. It was sculpted by Anthony Stones who lived in New Zealand from 1952 to 1983. He has also crafted several important statues in New Zealand. (See: Greenwich, London, and Gloucester) At the beginning of December the people of Derby commemorate this important event with a Bonnie Prince Charlie Parade and Battle. For details of the exact day each year, tel: (01332) 255802.

The defeat of Bonnie Prince Charlie's forces at Culloden in 1746 was the catalyst that destroyed the old clan system and ended the splendid isolation of the Highlands. This resulted in the rapid expansion of sheep flocks and the corresponding expulsion of the clansfolk from their ancestral lands – the notorious Highland Clearances.

However, out of this Scottish tragedy came a stroke of good fortune for New Zealand as thousands of Highlanders boarded the emigrant ships, thereby providing New Zealand with much of its early life blood. Had the subject of the statue here in Derby not turned around and marched his men to their doom at Culloden, the infusion of Scottish blood into New Zealand would not have been nearly so great.

No visit to Derby would be complete without a tour of the Royal Crown Derby Visitors' Centre at 194

Osmaston Road where one can see how Royal Crown Derby fine china is made. There is a museum and a factory shop where one can buy beautiful pieces at good prices.

The East Coast city of Gisborne takes its name from one of Derbyshire's most distinguished families who were mayors of Derby for two centuries - when these things were decided by birth rather than by ballot and the standard of local government was certainly no worse than it is to-day.

The particular member of the family after whom the New Zealand city was named was William Gisborne (1825-1898) who is regarded as the founder of the New Zealand public service. As Minister of Public Works in 1870 he had the important task of putting into effect the bold public works programme of Sir Julius Vogel which was responsible for lifting New Zealand out of the economic stagnation which had resulted from the Maori War of the 1860s.

William Gisborne (See: Rugby) must have been quite a character; when someone threw an orange at him during a ball in Auckland, he fought a duel with the miscreant. In 1881 he inherited Allestree Hall in Derbyshire from a cousin and returned to England to help manage the family estates.

Allestree Hall is situated in the village of Allestree, which is on the A6 on the northern outskirts of the city of Derby. It is not open to the public but one can walk through its 200 acre park. In fact, there is a special Allestree Park Nature Trail that starts and finishes in the car park which is only a few yards from the entrance to Allestree Hall.

The walk is just over one and a half miles in length and includes a lake and woodland which latter comprises oaks, beech, grey poplars, alders and yew trees. In the lake are mallards, Canada geese and a pair of Mute Swans, the largest British bird.

NOTTINGHAMSHIRE

For the New Zealand visitor Nottingham's two main attractions are Robin Hood and Trent Bridge. Not only is this famous cricket ground the venue for Test matches between New Zealand and England but also it was where New Zealand's greatest cricketer, Sir Richard Hadlee, spent ten years playing county cricket. In the 1984 season he achieved the remarkable feat of taking 100 wickets and scoring 1,000 runs, the 1,000th run being scored at Trent Bridge in front of his cheering home crowd.

One of the two new sports halls at Trent Bridge is called the Richard Hadlee Hall, the other being the Garry Sobers Hall. And in Trent Bridge's reception area, situated in the new Radcliffe Road Stand, is a photograph of New Zealand's finest cricketer. At Notts. Hadlee is remembered as not only one of its finest players but also one of the game's great gentlemen.

New Zealand's cricket links with Trent Bridge continued when Chris Cairns signed on with Notts. in 2001; he will find Richard Hadlee a hard act to follow.

LINCOLNSHIRE

Burghley House, Stamford Baron

For most New Zealanders the word "Burghley" means the Burghley Three-Day Horse Trials that take place in September in the grounds of Burghley House which have been dominated in recent years by New Zealand's greatest ever equestrian, Mark Todd. He won the event five times between 1987 and 1999.

The Three day Trials are based on horse events that were held on the Continent in the nineteenth century in order to test officers' chargers. On the first day the horses were on parade, the forerunner of the present Dressage test which is aimed at keeping the horse quiet, supple and obedient by systematic work.

On the second day the horses are tested across country as if they were carrying despatches from a commanding general to his forward troops. The third day is given over to showjumping to prove that the beasts are still sound and energetic after the strenuous tests of the previous day.

However, there is more to Burghley than the horse trials since Burghley House is the largest and finest surviving Elizabethan mansion in England.

More than nine hundred years ago Burghley Manor was leased to the chaplain of King Edward the Confessor. The Abbot of Peterborough built a monastery on the site in 1158 and part of it was incorporated into the current 240 roomed mansion that was erected here by William Cecil, the first Lord

Burghley (1520-98), when he was Lord High Treasurer to Elizabeth I and the most powerful man in the kingdom. His descendant, the Marquess of Exeter, is the current owner of Burghley House and its estate.

Inside the house can be seen the four poster bed where Elizabeth I slept when she stayed here. Another monarch who was a guest at Burghley was William III who thought that such a palace was far too grand for one of his subjects!

The surviving portions of the original monastery include the chapel, a splendid stone staircase and the kitchen, a huge vaulted room whose walls are covered with 260 ancient copper utensils as well as the skulls of many turtles which had been used to make soup for past banquets.

The Great Hall has a fine hammer beam roof while the walls of the Heaven Room were painted by Antonio Verrio, the talented seventeenth century Italian artist, and are one of the richest and most beautiful sights in England.

The nearest train station to Burghley House is Stamford. The park of Burghley is adjacent to the A1 highway. Burghley House is open to the public from 11 a.m. to 4.30 p.m. every day from 1st April to 31st October.

Lincoln

Situated on a hill overlooking the city, Lincoln Cathedral, with its three towers, is one of the grandest cathedrals in Christendom. Mostly built in the thirteenth

Lincoln Cathedral
In the Airmen's Chapel is a beautiful memorial window to the New Zealand airmen who died in the Second World War while serving with the Royal Air Force.

century, it is made of Lincolnshire limestone that was extracted from local quarries.

In the Airmen's Chapel is a memorial window to the New Zealand airmen who died in the Second World War while serving with the Royal Air Force. There were quite a few bomber squadrons based in the area and, as the pilots and crew took off on their nightly missions over Nazi occupied Europe, their last sight in the fading light was the great towers of Lincoln Cathedral which dominated the flat, surrounding countryside.

The memorial window was unveiled by Lord Freyberg V.C. on Battle of Britain Sunday, 1953. This former Governor-General reminded the gathering that, of the 11,000 New Zealanders who served in the Royal Air Force in Europe, some 3,318 lost their lives. They would be remembered, he said, "in the calm peace of this lovely Cathedral, where generations to come of young British people will linger here at this memorial, read their names and honour their memory".

Also in the Airmen's Chapel are books containing the names of 22,000 men of Nos 1 and 5 Bomber Groups and the 9th Training Group who were killed in the Second World War – including many New Zealanders. The books are stored in the wooden cabinet to the south of the altar and there is always one book with its pages open in the glass cabinet on the north wall.

South of the cathedral's Great West Door is a modern memorial to Sir Joseph Banks. There are guided tours of the cathedral which last approximately an hour.

A ceremony takes place in the cathedral every year on Battle of Britain Sunday, which is the Sunday closest to 15th September, the key day of the Battle of Britain. And, like the day of the Battle of Waterloo, the 15th of September in 1940 was a Sunday. Nothing like fighting in a righteous cause on the Lord's Day!

In front of the cathedral is Lincoln Castle which was built by William the Conqueror on the site of an earlier fortress that was established in A.D. 47 by the Ninth Legion of the Roman army.

In later centuries the Castle served as a prison; some of the inmates who were incarcerated here were transported to Australia.

The part of the Castle that served as a prison now houses one of only four surviving copies of Magna Carta, which is the foundation stone of the rights and freedoms of all the English speaking peoples. (See: Runnymede)

To-day Lincoln Castle is used for a variety of purposes – historical re-enactments, rock concerts and exhibitions by the Lincoln Castle Longbowmen – shades of the Age of Chivalry!

Behind the Castle is the area known as The Lawn where one can visit the Sir Joseph Banks Conservatory, a large glasshouse containing plants from some of the species that Banks brought back from Australia and New Zealand when he accompanied Captain Cook on the *Endeavour*.

CHESHIRE

Chester

Chester, a city known to the Romans, is dominated by its cathedral, a magnificent pile of red sandstone that varies in style from Norman to late Perpendicular. Situated right in the heart of Chester, the cathedral contains many memorials and relics of historical interest including a brass plaque in memory of Arthur Payne, first lieutenant on *H.M.S.Tauranga*, who was drowned in October, 1904, during a fierce gale off the coast of New Zealand "while in the execution of his duty".

LIVERPOOL

Liverpool was formerly one of the greatest ports in the world; before the First World War it had seven miles of docks on the Liverpool side of the Mersey and four miles on the other. It was also the largest port for the embarkation of emigrants to the colonies.

In the hundred years from 1830 to 1930 some nine million people emigrated from here to the United States, Canada, Australia, New Zealand and South Africa. Not all were British as people from Holland, Germany, Scandinavia, Poland and even Russia would sail to Hull on the east coast and then travel across to Liverpool by rail to board their vessel. The 13,000 mile voyage to New Zealand usually took about a hundred days and the fare was approximately £15 per person.

Almost a quarter of a million of New Zealand's settlers departed from this port.

Any New Zealander who wants to get some idea of the conditions under which one's forbears arrived in Liverpool from divers parts, there to board a cramped vessel for the long voyage to the other side of the world, the best place to visit is the "Emigrants to a New World" Gallery at the Merseyside Maritime Museum. This is situated at Liverpool's Albert Dock – close to the original "pool" of the Mersey which developed into Britain's largest port.

In the gallery can be seen a reconstruction of a nearby street where many of the emigrants lodged in cheap boarding houses while awaiting the call to board their vessel, thereby crossing the Rubicon as it were by severing their links with the Old World and throwing in their lot with the unknown lands that lay at the end of their voyage. Also on display in the gallery are posters advertising the departures of the emigrant ships, some trunks in which they carried their few possessions and even a reconstituted interior of an emigrant vessel, the *Shackamaxon*, which carried new settlers to America and Australia. Other exhibits are the original builder's model of the *Titanic*, a Liverpool registered vessel, and a nameplate from one of its lifeboats.

The Museum is open every day (except for a few days over Christmas) from 10.30 a.m. to 5.30 p.m. There is a restaurant and also a shop with a good selection of books and souvenirs. For those who want to search a little deeper there is the Maritime Archives and

Library on the Second Floor which has an extensive collection of books and documents.

Outside the Museum one can follow the Emigration Trail "Routes to the Roots". Details can be found in the Guidebook from the Museum.

On the trail can be seen the old red and white building that was the office of the White Star Line whose most famous ship was the *Titanic*. At the end of Pier Head is a monument to the engine room crew who perished when the *Titanic* hit the iceberg in 1912.

A short distance up Chapel Street from the Titanic memorial is a small pub called the *Pig and Whistle* which was where many of the emigrants to New Zealand had their last drink in England before answering the call to "Board ship". Inside the pub is an old brass plaque stating "Emigrants Supplied" – a relic of the days when emigrants had to provide their own food for the voyage and hostelries like the *Pig and Whistle* were able to supply their needs.

The best way to see Liverpool is to take a ferry from Pier Head "cross the Mersey" to Birkenhead. Ferries have been plying this route since the monks of Birkenhead Priory were granted a charter for the purpose in the fourteenth century. The Auckland suburb of Birkenhead was so named by Samuel Cochrane, an auctioneer who, when he looked out from his Auckland office across the Waitemata, was reminded of his home town of Liverpool with Birkenhead on the other side.

Liverpool has numerous places associated with the Beatles who made their one and only tour Down Under in the 1960s. And what did they think of little old New Zealand? John Lennon: "It reminds us of what Liverpool must have been like in the 1920s".

LANCASHIRE

Warrington

On the Sunday closest to Anzac Day there is an afternoon ceremony (4 p.m.) at Soldiers' Corner in the cemetery on Manchester Road, Warrington.

Saint Helens

Lancashire was the birth place of New Zealand's longest serving and greatest ever Prime Minister, Richard John Seddon.

Seddon was born on 22nd June, 1845, in the Old School House, Eccleston, on the outskirts of the industrial town of St. Helens. When his government established maternity homes in New Zealand, he named them Saint Helens Hospital, after the town where he was born while his home in Wellington, opposite Parliament, was called Eccleston Hill.

To-day the Old School House is a private residence but there is a plaque above the front door, recording Seddon's birth, which can be seen from the street. The Old School House is situated at No. 378 Prescot Road, between Broom Road and Seddon Road; the latter, of course, was named after the only man from St. Helens ever to become a Prime Minister.

Seddon worked on his grandfather's farm at Barrow Nook, Bickerstaffe, a small village north-west of St. Helens just off the A570. He used to visit there as a child but so noisy and destructive was he that, when he said to his grandfather, "I only wish we lived nearer so that I could come every day", the old man replied in his thick Lancashire accent, "Nay lad, thou livest plenty near enough and thou comes plenty often enough for my liking".

One of Seddon's earliest memories was as a school child assembled at Knowsley Hall, the ancestral home of the Earls of Derby, to sing the National Anthem when Queen Victoria paid a visit there.

In 1863 Seddon emigrated to Melbourne and a few years later he joined the gold rush to the West Coast of the South Island. It was there that he entered local politics and became a Member of Parliament. On the death of John Ballance in 1893 he became Prime Minister and died in harness in 1906. He was always both a man of the people and a staunch imperialist, believing that New Zealand benefitted from a strong and united British Empire. He once said that his two greatest problems as Prime Minister were "wine and women" by which he meant the issues of prohibition and women's suffrage.

Christ Church, in Church Lane, Eccleston, is easily identifiable by its spire and high pinnacles. The interior of the church contains an oak gallery and hammer-beam roof. There are also wooden choir stalls which were presented by Richard John Seddon's widow in 1908 in memory of her husband.

Saint Helens – Photograph: Mrs. Jane Aim
Entrance to the house where Richard John Seddon, Prime Minister 1893-1906, was born in 1845.

Further memorials to Seddon can be seen in the St. Helens Town Hall in Corporation Street where his portrait hangs on the wall of the Mayor's Parlour and his name is on the Roll of Freemen of the Borough. The latter is located in the public reception area of the Town Hall.

Lytham Saint Anne's

Lytham Saint Anne's (pronounced "Lithim" as in "rhythm") is a beach resort south of Blackpool. It has a special place in New Zealand golfing history for it was on its magnificent links that Bob Charles won the British Open in 1963. If you can do a round in 66, you will be matching Charles because that was his score in the Third Round when he equalled the course record.

MANCHESTER

For most New Zealanders Manchester means Coronation Street and Old Trafford and indeed no visit to this thriving city is complete without a tour of Granada Studios where Coronation Street is produced. Tel: (0161) 8329090.

It was at Manchester University that New Zealand's greatest genius, Ernest Rutherford, performed the first artificial splitting of the atom in 1918. At the time he was Professor of Physics at Manchester and there is a plaque in his honour at the university.

Church of St. John the Evangelist, Farsley, Leeds
In the church are seven stained glass windows in memory of Samuel Marsden who conducted the first Christian service in New Zealand on Christmas Day, 1814. Marsden was born in Farsley.

YORKSHIRE

Leeds

To the New Zealand ear Leeds means Headingley where the Black Caps have had their ups and downs in their matches against England.

However, Leeds has a much older connection with Down Under for Samuel Marsden, who introduced Christianity to New Zealand, was born in the village of Farsley in 1765. To-day Farsley is a suburb on the western edge of Leeds and is easily accessible from the Leeds ring road or via New Pudsey train station.

The house where Marsden was born in Town Street, the main street of Farsley, has been demolished and is now the Marsden memorial garden. Nearby in Town Street is the church of Saint John the Evangelist. Although built after Marsden left Farsley, it is the main memorial to him in England.

Built in 1843, the church's main feature is its tower which has a clock dial on its four sides so that they can be seen throughout the township. Inside the church seven stained glass windows (six of them in the chancel) commemorate his missionary activity in Australasia. Like Saint John, Marsden was an evangelist who took the Gospel to the farthest ends of the earth.

The windows depict the four Gospel-writers and the missionary journeys of Saint Paul; the central place is given to the figure of Christ as the Good Shepherd.

Another interesting feature of the church is its stone baptismal font. The skilled carving on the stone was done by a twelve year old apprentice, Alfred Bedford.

In the church yard near the porch is an obelisk in memory of the man who performed the first Christian service in New Zealand on Christmas Day, 1814. (See: Cambridge) At the back of the church is a Prayer Tree to which parishioners and visitors may attach a special prayer.

Services are held on Sundays at 9 a.m., 10.30 a.m. and 6.30 p.m. and on Wednesdays at 9.30 a.m. The church is usually open on Fridays and the first Saturday of each month from 10 a.m. to noon (coffee available in the Hall).

There are a few exhibits relating to Samuel Marsden in the Armley Mills Museum in Canal Road, Armley, which is two miles west of the Leeds city centre on the A65. Hours: Tuesday-Saturday, 10 a.m. to 5 p.m., Sundays, 1-5 p.m.

York

The ancient city of York is dominated by York Minster, which is the second most important church in the Anglican communion after Canterbury Cathedral. Apart from King's College Chapel, Cambridge, York Minster is the only major medieval church still to have its original windows. Towards the west end of the South Choir aisle is a memorial to the men of the 65th

(York and Lancaster) Regiment that commemorates its casualties in the Maori Wars between 1845 and 1866.

Beneath the towering walls of York Minster in High Petergate is the small church of Saint Michael-le-Belfry, which has an interesting connection with a popular tradition that is celebrated in both New Zealand and Britain – Guy Fawkes Day. It was in this church, originally a chapel for the private devotions of the Minster clergy, that Guy Fawkes was christened on 16th April, 1570. He was born just across the street from Saint Michael's in a house (now demolished) that stood behind the eighteenth century frontage of what is now the Guy Fawkes Tavern in High Petergate. An ideal place for a drink and, more importantly, a smoke; after all, smoke and fire is what Guy Fawkes is all about.

Born into an old and respected Yorkshire family, Guy Fawkes later went off the rails, fighting in the army of England's enemy, King Philip II of Spain, and being the lead man in the Gunpowder Plot of 5th November, 1605, to blow King and Parliament to kingdom come. But, if he hadn't "gone off the rails" his name would not be remembered four centuries later and millions of children would have been deprived of the pleasure of burning his effigy on the bonfire every Fifth of November and letting off fireworks. Nice one, Guy Fawkes!

Harrogate

The spa town of Harrogate, on the A59 west of York, is a sister city of Wellington. The links between

New Zealand and Harrogate go back to the Second World War when twenty-three New Zealand airmen, based in North Yorkshire, were buried at the Stonefall Cemetery, Wetherby Road, Harrogate. They are among the 994 graves of Commonwealth servicemen (mostly air crew) at Stonefall.

Although these young men lie far from home their graves have been tended by the Stonefall Adoption Committee of the Harrogate Victory Branch of the British Legion; each grave is cared for by a particular person who lays a poppy wreath at Christmas and at another time during the year as specified by the next-of-kin. A memorial service is held in the cemetery on the morning of the Sunday before Battle of Britain Sunday which, of course, is the Sunday closest to 15th September, the crux day of the Battle of Britain when the New Zealand commander, Air Vice-Marshal Park, skilfully used every operational plane in the British Isles to ward off the greatest air attack that Hitler launched against Britain.

In the Coronation Year of 1953 Harrogate City Council presented Wellington with a silver mace which is used on ceremonial occasions and at council meetings as a symbol of authority. It was given as a token of appreciation for the help that New Zealand gave to the Mother Country both during and after the Second World War.

Crafted by James Ogden and Sons, jewellers of Harrogate, it bears the coats-of-arms in enamel of both Wellington and Harrogate. In return Wellington gave an oil painting of its harbour and a collection of New

Zealand trees and shrubs which form the New Zealand Garden in the sheltered north-west corner of the Valley Gardens in the centre of Harrogate. The plants, representing dozens of native species, travelled to England in the vegetable room of the liner, *Dominion Monarch*, where they were looked after by the galley staff. In return Harrogate sent some of its rose bushes to the Lady Norwood Rose Garden in Wellington.

In 1978 Wellington established its first ever "sister-city" relationship with Harrogate to commemorate the special links between them.

Captain Cook Country

Yorkshire is, of course, Captain Cook country and there are several places in the East Riding of that unique county that have associations with the great navigator who discovered New Zealand. We will deal with these according to the chronology of Cook's life rather than in any geographical order.

For the really serious Captain Cook followers there is the Captain Cook Heritage Trail which follows the route Whitby-Guisborough-Great Ayton-Marton-Morton-Guisborough-Marske-Staithes-Whitby.

Marton, Middlesborough

Cook was born on 27th October, 1728, in a thatched two-roomed labourer's cottage in the village of Marton. In Cook's time Marton was a small village of only a few houses; to-day it is part of the south-eastern sprawl of the industrial town of Middlesborough. It is no longer possible to see this house as it has been pulled down. There is, however, a granite vase that marks the site. It is situated only a few yards from the Captain Cook Birthplace Museum in Stewart Park where an effigy of Cook can be seen on board a model of the *Endeavour*.

On 3rd November, 1728, Cook was baptised in the local church of Saint Cuthbert's at Ormesby, a short distance to the east of Stewart Park. When this church was later rebuilt a piece of sandstone with dogtooth carvings was saved and sent out to New Zealand where it sits in Holy Trinity Church at Gisborne, less than a mile from the spot where Cook first landed in New Zealand. In the rebuilt church of Saint Cuthbert's are stained glass windows celebrating Cook's life and a copy of his baptismal entry in the register.

The farming town of Marton in the Rangitikei was so named after Cook's birthplace in 1869, which was the centenary of his discovery of New Zealand in 1769.

In the Cleveland Centre, opposite Middlesborough's Town Hall, is a model of the *Endeavour* and a tiled floor showing a map of the great navigator's voyages.

West of Middlesborough is the industrial town of Stockton-on-Tees where there is a full-size replica of the Endeavour at the Castlegate Quay Heritage Centre on the River Tees.

When Cook was eight years old the family left Marton and moved five miles away to the village of Great Ayton.

Great Ayton

On the summit of Easby Moor, south-west of Great Ayton, stands an obelisk in honour of the village's most famous son. Cook, who was to become one of the great scientific minds of the age, attended the Old School which to-day is the Captain Cook Schoolhouse Museum. In 1997 a statue of Cook as a boy was unveiled. It was crafted by Nicholas Dimbleby.

At Great Ayton's All Saints church are buried Captain Cook's mother and five of his brothers and sisters.

Cook left here when he was thirteen to be apprenticed to a grocer at Staithes but his parents remained in Great Ayton and later built a two storey brick cottage. It was later dismantled and taken out to Melbourne where it was re-erected in Fitzroy Gardens on the occasion of Melbourne's centenary in 1934. Every nail was carefully marked and even the mortar between the bricks was collected in bags and transported to Australia. Cook never lived in this cottage as, by the time his parents built it, he had joined the Navy. However, it is likely that he visited it while on leave. The site of this cottage in Bridge Street, Great Ayton, is marked by a rock that was brought over from Port Hicks, the first point of land that he sighted in Australia. In other words, Australia got a whole cottage from Great Ayton and all that Great Ayton got in return was a piece of rock.

Staithes

This once busy fishing port and smuggling centre on the A174 north of Whitby was where Captain Cook got his first glimpse of the sea; from the age of thirteen he was apprenticed to a grocer whose shop was just around the corner from the Cod and Lobster Inn which can be seen on the foreshore by the river mouth. However, the grocer's shop no longer exists as it was washed away by the sea, this part of the Yorkshire coast being particularly prone to erosion. Even the Cod and Lobster has been washed away three times but has always been rebuilt. Some of the materials from the original grocer's shop were recovered and used to help build the present "Cook's shop" in Staithes.

At Staithes, to-day a much quieter place than in Cook's day, one can visit the Captain Cook and Staithes Heritage Centre, a converted Methodist chapel which contains exhibits on Cook's life here in Staithes.

Cook's boss was a hard taskmaster so young James ran away from here to the much bigger port of Whitby where he signed on as a cabin-boy and, as they say, the rest is history. He is believed to have taken a shilling from the grocery till to finance his flight. It might be a good idea to drop into the Cod and Lobster and drink a toast to the mean old boss. Why? Because, if he was a kinder employer Cook might have stayed, in which case Australia and New Zealand would not have been discovered and taken under the wing of Britain in the way that they were. By Gad, we could even be speaking French! Or Russian!

Whitby

When Cook arrived in Whitby at the age of eighteen he was apprenticed to Messrs. Walker, a firm of Whitby shipowners whose vessels were carrying coal from Newcastle to London and it was here that he learnt his first lessons in the art of seamanship. He sailed on these sturdily built colliers before joining the Navy in 1755 as an able seaman.

One can visit the seventeenth century red-brick house in Grape Lane beside the River Esk, which flows into Whitby's harbour, where Cook lived for three years during his nine year apprenticeship. This is now the Captain Cook Memorial Museum. It was the home of young James' master, Captain John Walker, a Quaker shipowner; when not on board one of Walker's colliers sailing between Newcastle and London, Cook and the other apprentice seamen lodged in the attic.

It is possible for the visitor to stand at the window of the attic and look out across the waters of the harbour as Cook used to – all the way to the sea that was to take him to the ends of the earth, further than any man had ever gone before – in fact, all the way to New Zealand. On the other side of the River Esk were the yards where Cook's ships were built.

The Captain Cook Memorial Museum is open from April to the end of October, 9.45 a.m. – 5.p.m. In

Captain Cook's attic.
Photograph: Capt. Cook Memorial Museum, Whitby
The attic in the Captain Cook Memorial Museum, Whitby, where the great navigator slept and studied.

March it is open week-ends only at the same hours. There is a small gift shop.

Whitby Museum, in Pannet Park on the other side of the river, has a special section on the life of Captain Cook and there is a statue of him on the West Cliff where he gazes seawards across the harbour mouth. This was unveiled in 1968, which was the bicentenary of his setting out on his first voyage to the Pacific. The inscription reads: "For the lasting memory of a great Yorkshire seaman this bronze has been cast and is left in the keeping of Whitby, the birthplace of those good ships that bore him on his enterprises, brought him glory and left him at rest".

In Cook's time Whitby, with a population of about 5,000, was the centre of a large whaling industry and some 2,761 whales were brought ashore here between 1753 and 1833. It also had a vibrant shipbuilding industry.

Whitby's traditions as a Christian settlement and whaling port go back a very long way and it was here in 664 A.D. that the Synod of Whitby determined the (moving) date of Easter.

A few years later Saint Hilda, a Northumbrian princess, founded a community for monks and nuns here. The eye catching ruins of Whitby Abbey on top of the cliff dominate the town and its historic harbour.

The settlement of Whitby, north of Wellington, is named after this historic port and all its street names have associations with Cook. Whitby, Yorks, is also a "twin town" of Whitianga on the shores of Mercury Bay. This is an obvious relationship since Captain Cook spent eleven days in Mercury Bay on his first voyage. He found it a convenient place to observe the transit of Mercury, which enabled him to establish his longitude; hence its name. Cook also took on fresh water from the nearby streams, cleaned the ship and surveyed the district. He and his crew found delectable rock oysters up a stream as well as wild fowl and wild celery. Before leaving on 15th November, 1769, the great navigator carved the ship's name and date on a tree, hoisted the flag and took possession of the place in the name of George III.

DURHAM

Durham

"Grey towers of Durham!...
Well yet I love thy mixed and massive piles,
Half church of God, half castle 'gainst the Scot;
And long to roam these venerable aisles,
With records stored of deeds long since forgot."

- Sir Walter Scott, *Harold the Dauntless*, 1817

The city of Durham is dominated by the towers of its castle and Romanesque cathedral, which dates from the eleventh century. Standing on its own peninsula the cathedral is surrounded by the River Wear. The best views of this magnificent structure are from either the Prebends' Bridge or the paths along the river. Inside the cathedral is the impressive memorial to the Durham Light Infantry; included on its list of campaigns is "New Zealand".

The 68th (Durham Light Infantry) Regiment arrived in New Zealand from Burma in 1864 to fight in the Maori War. For the next two years it was involved in regular battles and skirmishes, the most famous of which was at Gate Pa near Tauranga.

Encamped in the clover fields while protecting the Te Papa mission, the men from Durham built what was known as the Durham Redoubt on the site of what is now Durham Street in Tauranga. They watched as the Maoris built a pa nearby and then they attacked it. Their commanding officer was Lt. Col. Greer after whom the Tauranga suburb of Greerton, the site of Gate Pa, was named.

The 68th moved silently and in single file through the dark to take up positions at the rear of the pa while other troops stormed it from the front at daybreak. When the 68th fired from the rear there was great confusion and the storming troops began to retire in disorder.

In the confusion and gunsmoke the Maoris managed to escape through the extended lines of the Durham Light Infantry, only to be re-engaged and defeated at nearby Te Ranga a short time later.

Te Ranga ended the Maori resistance in the Bay of Plenty; shortly afterwards some 133 leading Maoris, including many chiefs, came to Tauranga to make their submission to Lt. Col. Greer and peace has reigned in the Bay of Plenty ever since. In the words of one writer,

"Tranquillity settled once more on Tauranga. The 68th took out their cricket stumps again while the war went on in the west."

The men from this Durham regiment sailed from New Zealand in 1866 and disembarked at Portsmouth, England. In 1881 the 68th became the 1st Battalion of the Durham Light Infantry.

Approximately a mile from the cathedral (through the city) is the Durham Light Infantry Museum at Aykley Heads. It is well sign-posted. Among its exhibits is a water-colour of Te Kuha, New Zealand, by Lieutenant H.G.Robley and an old bottle which Private Hughes of the Durham Light Infantry threw overboard as his battalion sailed from Southampton to France in 1914. He was killed twelve days later. The bottle, containing a message to his wife, was discovered by a British fisherman at the mouth of the Thames in 1998; it hadn't travelled very far in 84 years!

As a result of publicity in a national newspaper Private Hughes' daughter, Mrs. Emily Crowehurst, was located in New Zealand and the bottle was presented to her by the fisherman. Mrs. Crowehurst then travelled to Durham and presented the bottle and message to the Lord Lieutenant of Durham as trustee for the Museum at a ceremony during the Durham Light Infantry reunion week-end.

In the Museum's Medal Room can be seen the medals of Sergeant John Murray V.C. During the battle of Te Ranga he rescued Corporal Byrne who was about to be killed by a tomahawk wielding Maori. For his feat Murray was awarded the Victoria Cross, the same decoration that Corporal Byrne had won in the Crimean War. It is on display with his other medals and is one of the few Victoria Crosses ever awarded for action in New Zealand.

Bishop Auckland

Situated on the River Wear twelve miles south of Durham on the A688 is the market town from which New Zealand's largest city indirectly takes its name. The town of Bishop Auckland dates back to Roman times when it was a fort to guard the great road which they constructed to link York with Hadrian's Wall. The only part of the fort that is visible to-day is the underground heating chamber.

Bishop Auckland is the official residence of the Bishop of Durham. The bishops of this northern see formerly lived in Durham Castle but, when that was taken over by Durham University in 1836, they moved here to the castle at Bishop Auckland. The grounds of the 800 acres of the episcopal residence are open to the public.

George Eden, the first Earl of Auckland (1784-1849), who was Governor-General of India from 1836 to 1841, took his title from Bishop Auckland. Before sailing out to India as Queen Victoria's representative on the sub-continent, Auckland was First Lord of the Admiralty in London in which capacity he gave Captain Hobson the command of *HMS Rattlesnake* for his expedition to New Zealand. When Hobson sailed past Rangitoto and into the harbour he named the future city in honour of his naval patron who was by then the Viceroy of India.

It was in honour of the Earl of Auckland's family name of Eden that the suburbs of Mount Eden and Glen Eden were named as well as Eden Park. Sir Anthony Eden, Prime Minister of Great Britain from 1955 to 1957, was also a member of this distinguished family. And so it was that Auckland was named after the man who was Governor-General of India while he in turn took his title from Auckland (now called Bishop Auckland) in this part of Durham.

A little to the south-west is a tiny village built around a large green. Its name: West Auckland. A far cry from the sprawling suburbia of West Auckland, New Zealand!

Sunderland

On the A183 south-west of Sunderland is a prominent memorial to John Lambton, the first Earl of Durham. New Zealand has cause to be thankful to this man for two reasons. First, as chairman of the New Zealand Company he was instrumental in arranging the departure of the *Tory* in 1839 which led to the founding of Wellington. On Saturday, 27th April, 1839, he presided at a farewell dinner in London for the ship and he inspected her before she sailed.

When the *Tory* entered Wellington harbour in September, 1839, Colonel William Wakefield, the Resident-General of the Company in New Zealand and brother of Edward Gibbon Wakefield, named it

Lambton Harbour after the family name of the Earl of Durham. Lambton Quay, which then skirted the foreshore, was similarly named.

The second reason to be grateful to Durham was because, as Governor-General of Canada, he provided it with a format for responsible government which was later followed in the Australian colonies and New Zealand, leading to the fully independent status under which all three countries thrive to-day.

The monument to this far-sighted man, known as "Radical Jack" for his progressive views, stands on Penshaw Hill and is in the shape of a roofless Doric temple. From its eminence can be obtained an excellent view of the area.

South Shields

South Shields, on the southern bank of the Tyne, was the birthplace of one of New Zealand's earliest Premiers who had a considerable influence on the development of the country in its formative years. Sir William Fox was born at Westoe in 1812. His birthplace, a fine Georgian house, is now the Sir William Fox Hotel and his portrait can be seen in the bar. The hotel is mainly devoted to accommodation although members of the public may enjoy drinks in the bar.

After being called to the Bar at the Inner Temple, London, in 1842 William Fox emigrated to New Zealand where he was an explorer, painter, Prime Minister and prohibitionist. In 1843 he was a member of the first party of white men to enter the Wairarapa and he painted landscapes of both that area and Nelson.

Like Wakefield he was a great believer in organised colonisation. He called the Treaty of Waitangi "shallow, flimsy sophistry", arguing that Maoris had rights only to the lands they actually inhabited and cultivated and not to the whole country.

Fox fought strenuously for the right of self-government for New Zealand, often pitting his first class brain and debating skills against the Colonial Office in London. Both the Fox Glacier and the town of Foxton, north of Wellington, are named after this man of many parts.

In view of the present trade carried on at his birthplace the most interesting aspect of Fox's career was his founding of the New Zealand Alliance, the main prohibitionist organisation that sought to outlaw all alcoholic beverages. Enough for a thirsty guest to order a triple at the Sir William Fox Hotel!

Newcastle

In the north-west Transept of Newcastle's cathedral in Saint Nicholas Street is a bust of Admiral Collingwood who took over command of the British fleet in the Battle of Trafalgar when Nelson died of his wounds and after whom the town of Collingwood in Golden Bay, N.Z. is named. The admiral was baptised and married in this cathedral. (See: Saint Paul's Cathedral, London, and Tynemouth)

NORTHUMBERLAND

Tynemouth

At the mouth of the river at Tynemouth is a huge monument to Admiral Collingwood who, as we have seen, gave his name to the town of Collingwood at the top of the South Island. A fine view can be enjoyed from the top. (See: Saint Paul's Cathedral, London, and Newcastle). Situated at Spanish Battery, it is next to the Volunteer Lifeboat Museum. Whenever a Royal Navy ship enters the Tyne its ship's company stands on deck and salutes this monument to the hero of Trafalgar.

Near Tynemouth's Fish Quay is Dockway Square in which stands a statue of Stan Laurel of Laurel and Hardy; he was brought up here.

Warkworth

The town of Warkworth in Northland was named after the seaside village of Warkworth on the Northumberland coast by its founder, John Anderson Brown, who came from Northumberland. The name "Warkworth" derives from the twelfth century Anglo-Saxon word "Wercewode" which means the enclosure or homestead of a woman called Werce. She was an abbess who gave a sheet of fine linen to the Venerable Bede to be used as his shroud. Warkworth is thirty-three miles north of Newcastle-upon-Tyne on the A1068. The two Warkworths at the opposite ends of the earth are twin towns and on the night of the Millennium they

Warkworth Castle
The town of Warkworth, North Auckland, was named after this castellated settlement in Northumberland. On the night of the Millennium the two towns exchanged greetings.

exchanged messages, the people of the English town holding a torchlight procession in freezing temperatures around their medieval village.

Some of the streets in the New Zealand town of Warkworth are named after prominent families of Nortumberland – the Percys (Dukes of Northumberland), the Nevilles, Bertrams, and Lilburns, while others take their names from villages near Warkworth, U.K. – Alnwick, Morpeth, Hexham and Bambro, not forgetting, of course, Coquet Street which is named after the river that flows through the English town. Nor is the Northumberland town of Warkworth without its New Zealand connections; in its beautiful 1,265 year old church is a memorial to a local man who was killed at the battle of Gate Pa during the Maori War.

One enters Warkworth, Northumberland, over a medieval bridge that is guarded by an ancient gatehouse. The church and castle dominate opposite ends of the main street. The church, which stands close beside the River Coquet, is of sandstone and its origins date from King Coelwulf's reign in the eighth century. However, the present church building, with its beautiful vaulted chancel, is Norman of the twelfth and thirteenth centuries.

At the top of the hill can be seen the ruins of Warkworth Castle. With a steep drop to the river on its western side and the sea on the other side it was ideal for defensive purposes. Its most striking features are the polygonal turrets, which are characteristic of the thirteenth century although the castle was, in fact, built

two centuries earlier. From 1322 it was the stronghold of the Percys, the Earls (later Dukes) of Northumberland. It was at Warkworth Castle that the Earl of Northumberland heard of the death in battle of his son, Hotspur. Shakespeare wrote of this incident in *Henry IV*:
"So did our men, heavy in Hotspur's loss,
Lend to this weight such lightness with their fear".

The best way to see the castle is to take a boat trip along the thickly wooded course of the river. This ruined castle is open to the public.

Howick

Three miles from Warkworth is the tiny village of Howick off the B1339. Half a mile from the village is Howick Hall which has been the home of the Grey family since 1319. Earl Grey (of the tea!) was Prime Minister of England from 1830 to 1834 and is best remembered for introducing the Reform Bill of 1832 which extended the franchise to the middle classes. Earl Grey's son bore the title of Lord Howick before he succeeded his father as the 3rd Earl Grey. The Auckland suburb of Howick is named after him.

When he was Secretary of State for the Colonies he was asked by the Governor of New Zealand, Sir George Grey (no relation) for troops to defend the Auckland settlers against attacks by Hone Heke. Earl Grey's response was to send out a permanent force of military veterans from Britain. These soldier-settlers, known as the Royal New Zealand Fencibles, were the original colonists of Howick, Auckland. (See: Gravesend) They had to be men of good character, no more than 48 years old and at least five feet, five inches in height. The memorial to the third Earl Grey – a gravestone and plaque – can be seen at Saint Michael's church in the grounds.

The present house at Howick, Northumberland, was rebuilt in 1926 after a fire. It has extensive gardens which have been planted with trees from all over the world. Many of the trees in the Long Walk were planted by the second Earl Grey who, apart from being Prime Minister and fathering sixteen children, seems to have had plenty of spare time for gardening. One of his daughters married John Lambton, the first Earl of Durham after whom Wellington's Lambton Quay was named (See: Sunderland, Durham) Howick is very much a "gardener's garden"; it concentrates on the plants and avoids the theme park attractions of other country houses.

The gardens of Howick Hall (but not the House) are open to the public. Hours: Early April-late October – daily from 1 p.m. to 6 p.m.

SCOTLAND

Since almost half the population of New Zealand are of Scottish descent it shouldn't be too difficult relating to the "guid folk" north of the Tweed – shared names, shared values and, up to a point, a shared language. On this last point one is reminded of the Englishman who was transferred to Glasgow and shortly afterwards was called up for jury service; at the end of the first week of the lengthy trial he stood up and asked the judge if he could be excused from the rest of the trial "because I haven't understood a single word that anyone has said all week".

To make it easier for New Zealand clansfolk to trace their backgrounds I list below some of the Clan museums and heritage centres.

Cameron: The Clan Cameron Museum, Achnacarry, near Spean Bridge, Invernesshire. From Fort William take the A82 north, then turn on to the B8005 and then on to the small, private road to Achnacarry. Opening hours: April-October, every day from 1.30 p.m. – 5 p.m. In July and August the times are 11 a.m. to 5 p.m.

Campbell: See Inveraray Castle, Argyll. Hours: From first Saturday in April to second Sunday in October, Monday-Saturday, 10 a.m. - 1 p.m. and 2 p.m. - 5.45 p.m., Sundays, 1 p.m.-5.45 p.m.

Gunn: Clan Gunn Heritage Centre and Museum, Latheron, on the A99 south of Wick. Hours: June-September, Monday-Saturday, 11 a.m. – 1 p.m. and 2 – 4 p.m. In July and August it is open on Sundays, 2 – 4 p.m.

MacAlister: Glenbarr Abbey, Glenbarr, 12 miles north of Campbeltown on the A83. Hours: April-October, 10 a.m. – 6 p.m. Closed Tuesday.

MacDonald: Clan Donald Centre, Armadale Castle, Armadale, Sleat, Isle of Skye. (See: Skye) Hours: April-October, every day from 9 a.m. to 5.30 p.m.

MacPherson: Clan MacPherson Museum, Main Street, Newtonmore. Hours: March-October, 10 a.m. – 5.30 p.m.

Menzies: Menzies Castle, Aberfeldy, Perthshire.

Sutherland: Clan Sutherland Society, Clan Room, Dunrobin Castle (near Golspie on the A9 north of Inverness).

DUMFRIES

Gretna Green

Driving north from Carlisle on the A74, the first town across the Scottish border is Gretna Green, which was famous for its "quickie" marriages for eloping couples from England. They used to nip over the border to take advantage of the Scottish law which, unlike England's, did not require marriage banns to be read out in a church but only a declaration before a witness. And in Scotland the parents' permission was not needed for people aged sixteen or above whereas in England the age was older.

These easy marriages usually took place at an inn. From 1826 the village blacksmith became the most popular man to perform the "ceremony".

One of the smithy's marriages had an important effect on the history of New Zealand. Edward Gibbon Wakefield abducted a wealthy heiress, Ellen Turner, and spirited her to Gretna Green where they were married in a quick ceremony by the ever obliging blacksmith cum marriage celebrant who was only too happy to add a marriage fee to his normal income from shoeing horses.

Wakefield and his young bride fled to France. However, they were pursued and overtaken at Calais and the rather shaken girl was taken back to England by her relatives while the marriage was annulled and Wakefield was sentenced to three years in Newgate Prison in London.

Fortunately for New Zealand he put his time in gaol to good use and conceived a grand plan of colonisation whereby all classes would be utilised to start new colonies instead of mostly convicts and riff raff as had hitherto been the case in Australia.

Under the "Wakefield system" land would be sold by the colonising association (the New Zealand Company, the Canterbury Association, etc.) at a sufficiently high price and would be released only as it was needed so as to prevent speculation. Settlement would be concentrated with relatively small farms and the profits from the land sales would be used to bring out more immigrants from the British Isles.

The policy had the twin aims of opening up new agricultural land in New Zealand and accommodating the surplus British farmers and agricultural labourers who were being dispossessed by the enclosure of common land in the Old Country.

Although there were variants to the system when it got going, Wakefield's scheme was responsible for getting New Zealand under way as a settled British colony based on agriculture. It was applied in its purest form in Canterbury with the result that that province became the most successful and prosperous area of New Zealand.

Gretna Green was what triggered Wakefield's spell behind bars and that in turn gave him the time to conceive a successful scheme of colonisation. So, if you are passing through Gretna Green, why not stop at one of the inns and drink a toast to the naughty blacksmith for his role in getting New Zealand going.

Carsethorne

This small fishing village on the lower Nith estuary (just off the A710 south of Dumfries) was the last place in Scotland that was seen by many of the emigrants to New Zealand. Its ruined jetty stands as a silent reminder of the thousands of Scots who boarded their vessels here for the uncomfortable voyage to the other end of the world. In 1850 alone some 4,000 left from this small jetty for a better life in New Zealand.

AYRSHIRE

"O Ayr, my dear, native ground."

- Robert Burns

Mossgiel

Ayrshire on the west coast of Scotland is best known as being the home of the Scottish bard, Robbie Burns. The town of Mosgiel, on the southern edge of Dunedin, was named after the Ayrshire farm of Mossgiel where Burns lived for four years. It was during this time that he wrote some of his most memorable poems.

Burns' brother, Gilbert, was also born at Mossgiel and it was his son, Rev. Thomas Burns (1796-1871), who was one of the two leaders who brought the Presbyterian settlers out from Scotland to establish the town of Dunedin.

The old farmhouse is no longer there but the site can be seen from the road. Travelling north-east from Ayr to Tarbolton, take the A744 and follow the signs towards Mauchline. The road winds its way along the top of a ridge and there are some wonderful views that would have been familiar to Burns.

When Mauchline comes into view one can see the farm, which is now called East Mossgiel. The hedge in front of the private house is said to have been planted by Robbie and Gilbert Burns.

Riccarton

Also in Ayrshire is the village of Riccarton, which is now a suburb of Kilmarnock. This was where Canterbury's first runholders, the Deans brothers, John and William, grew up and they named their farm on the Canterbury Plains "Riccarton" in honour of their native parish. It is now a suburb of Christchurch. In 1914 the Deans family presented the "Riccarton bush", the last patch of native forest in the area, to the city of Christchurch. They also named Christchurch's river after the Avon, a small brook on the border of Ayrshire and Lanarkshire where they used to play in their boyhood.

It was a good thing for New Zealand rugby that the Deans brothers decided to leave Ayrshire and settle in Canterbury; among their descendants have been Bob Deans, who scored the famous try against Wales in 1905 that was disallowed (See: Cardiff) and more recently, Bruce and Robbie Deans, who have contributed so much to Canterbury and All Black teams.

Kelburn Castle

On the scenic coast of North Ayrshire is Kelburn Castle which has been the home of the Boyle family since 1140. It is one of the oldest inhabited castles in Scotland. Its site was chosen for its commanding position overlooking the Firth of Clyde and its proximity to fresh water – the Kel burn ("mountain stream").

The original thirteenth century Norman keep is now enclosed within the walls of a larger castle, which was built in 1581. The head of the family, David Boyle, became the first Earl of Glasgow in 1703; it was he who added the mansion house on to the existing castle. This includes the drawing room, reputed to be one of the most beautiful rooms in Scotland.

The 7th Earl of Glasgow was Governor of New Zealand from 1892 to 1897. Always a keen walker, he was often seen in tweeds, tan boots and a stout walking stick hiking around Wellington's windy hills. His daughter, Alice, later married Sir Charles Fergusson, who would also be Governor-General of New Zealand. There are several portraits of him at Kelburn Castle.

Kelburn in Wellington was named after his son and heir, Viscount Kelburn, who, of course, took his title from the mountain stream that runs through a succession of gorges and waterfalls on the family estate while Wellington's Glasgow Wharf was named after the Earl.

When he returned to Kelburn Castle from the Antipodes the Earl built a corrugated iron building to house all the artefacts that he had been presented with in New Zealand. To-day this Museum is open to the public and contains photographs and other exhibits from New Zealand.

The Earl also brought back a number of trees and shrubs which are planted in the walled New Zealand Garden, which is not open to the public. At

Kelburn they thrived in a climate that is both damp but also surprisingly warm because of the Gulf Stream that passes up the west coast of Scotland on its way from the Gulf of Mexico. New Zealand flax bushes can be seen around the pond by the Museum and also in the Plaisance ("pleasant place"), the walled garden below the forecourt.

The Plaisance is dominated by two yew trees, a male and a female, which are more than a thousand years old. They would have been seen by the soldiers who fought in the Battle of Largs on the seashore below in 1263. This combat betweeen the Scots and the Norwegians resulted in the deaths of 16,000 Norwegians and 5,000 Scots. This Scottish victory put an end to the Norse hegemony over the Highlands. Among the surviving Scottish soldiers were the ancestors of many New Zealanders whose more immediate forbears were evicted from their lands in the Highland Clearances and sailed to a new life in New Zealand.

Next to the Plaisance is a Children's Garden that is in the shape of the Scottish flag. Alongside the Children's Garden is a weeping larch, a single tree that covers a quarter of an acre of ground!

There are woodland walks on each side of the Kel Burn, which drops seven hundred feet by way of waterfalls and deep gorges. The wildlife that can be seen on these walks includes roe deer, foxes, grey herons, long tail tits, bullfinches and swallows. There is also pony trekking, an adventure course (built with the help of the Royal Marines), a stockade and a Secret

Forest that contains a grotto, crocodile swamp, wooden maze, gingerbread house and pagoda.

Kelburn Castle and Country Park is situated on the A78 between Fairlie and Largs. The nearest station is Largs, two miles away, and there is a free minibus service from the station to the castle.

When not reserved for private functions Kelburn Castle is open for guided tours every afternoon from 30th June to 9th September. Group tours can be arranged at other times of the year if booked in advance. To check if the castle is closed because of a private function, telephone (01475) 568685.

The Kelburn Country Centre is open daily 10 a.m. – 6 p.m. from the beginning of April to the end of October. During the rest of the year the grounds are open from 11 a.m. to 5 p.m. (or dusk) every day except Christmas Day, Boxing Day and New Year's Day.

Kilbirnie

A few miles west of Kelburn Castle on the A760 is the town of Kilbirnie, the birth place of James Coutts Crawford, a pioneer of Wellington who bought the Miramar peninsula which was later subdivided into the suburbs of Miramar, Seatoun and Kilbirnie, the last mentioned of which was named after his home town here in Ayrshire. His own name is remembered in Wellington's Mount Crawford.

RENFREWSHIRE

Greenock

Greenock, on the south bank of the Firth of Clyde, was an important embarkation point for thousands of Scots who emigrated to New Zealand. It was from here that the first Scottish settlers sailed to Wellington. A hundred and twenty of them left on the *Bengal Merchant* which arrived in Wellington Harbour in February, 1840 – just as the settlement was being moved from Petone to the less windy and better drained site at Thorndon.

GLASGOW

"The Clyde made Glasgow and Glasgow made the Clyde".

- Old saying of Glaswegians

The great city of Glasgow is situated on the river Clyde whose waters have wetted many an anchor of emigrant ships as they set sail for New Zealand. These included the *Duchess of Argyle* and *Jane Gifford* which left here on 9th June, 1842, en route for the distant port of Auckland. The passengers on board were nothing less than the founding bloodstock of New Zealand's largest city.

The Clyde gave its name to an important river in the South Island. The Clutha was named by early

Scottish settlers, the word "Cluth" being the old Gaelic word for the Clyde. The town of Clyde in Central Otago is on the east bank of the Clutha River while Balclutha, also on the river and originally known as "Clutha" Ferry, is simply the Gaelic word for "village on the Clyde".

Alumni of Otago University might feel a sense of *déjà vu* when they see the buildings of Glasgow University at Gilmorehill overlooking Kelvingrove Park. The design of Otago, which was built in 1878 and is the oldest university in New Zealand, was based on that of Glasgow which had been built eight years earlier to the plans of the eminent architect, Sir George Gilbert Scott. To have built such an elaborate university in New Zealand at such an early stage is testimony to the high value that the Scots have always put on education. And, in a reversal of the usual trend of British place names finding their way to New Zealand, the street running off Kelvingrove Park to the north is called Otago Street. The street sign is a good photo op for those who come from the deep south.

Glasgow's Gothic cathedral has its origins in a wattle and daub cell that Saint Mungo built on the site in A.D. 543. Its most interesting feature is its oak pulpit with an hour-glass in front of it; it takes thirty-eight minutes for the sand to pass through the tiny hole. This is meant to be the limit of a sermon's length but some loquacious preachers have been known to turn it up the other way after thirty-eight minutes and keep going. It was from this pulpit that Donald Cargill, the Covenanting minister who was executed for denouncing Charles II, used to preach. His descendant, Captain William Cargill, was a co-founder of the Otago settlement and the town of Invercargill is named after him.

DUNBARTONSHIRE

Rosneath

The Wellington suburb of Roseneath is the anglicised form of the Gaelic word "Rossinath" which means "promontory of the sanctuary" – an appropriate name for the peninsula of Rosneath in Dunbartonshire which is flanked by the waters of the Gare Loch and the Clyde for in olden times it was a place for burying the dead (sanctuary).

Dominated by its great palace the Rosneath peninsula is opposite the port of Greenock from which so many emigrant ships sailed to New Zealand. To get there by car, take the A814 north-west from Glasgow and then turn off on the B833.

It was felt that the peninsula at the foot of Mount Victoria which juts into Wellington harbour bore a resemblance to the Rosneath peninsula in Scotland which was praised by Sir Walter Scott in *Heart of Midlothian* for its natural beauty. Hence the name.

EDINBURGH

"Stately Edinburgh throned on crags."

- Wordsworth, *The Excursion*, 1834

When Dunedin was founded in 1848 as a Scottish Free Church settlement the original intention was to call it "New Edinburgh". However, at the suggestion of the publisher of dictionaries, Sir William Chambers, who was then Lord Provost (Mayor) of Edinburgh, it was instead given the more original and romantic Celtic name of Dun Edin (literally: "Edinburgh on the hill"). Edinburgh in Scotland is believed to derive its name from Edwin, who became king of Northumbria in 617 A.D. (Edwin's Town). A statue of William Chambers stands in Chambers Street, Edinburgh.

There was a general instruction from the New Zealand Company that the new town, that was being staked out as the capital of Otago, should reproduce as far as possible the features of its Scottish parent city but differences in topography were to make this difficult. Although Dunedin copied some important Edinburgh street names – Princes Street, George Street, High Street, Castle Street, Saint Andrews Street, Hanover Street, Frederick Street, Saint David Street, Albany Street, Moray Place and Canongate – the layout is quite different.

The foundation stone of the lookout on Signal Hill, Dunedin, contains a piece of rock from Edinburgh Castle.

A further link between the two cities was established during the dark days of 1943 when the Mayor of Dunedin, Mr. A.H.Allen, organised a public fund for the people of Edinburgh. Some £1,000 was raised and, when it was received in Edinburgh, the Lord Provost used it to create a "Dunedin Room", with panels of New Zealand rimu, in the Edinburgh City Chambers.

In the Dunedin Room are several paintings of Dunedin by New Zealand artists, including Peter McIntyre, Graham Tait, Douglas Chowus and K. John Toomer.

In view of all these close links it was inevitable that Dunedin and Edinburgh would formalise their relationship and in 1974 they became "sister-cities".

The main feature of Edinburgh is, of course, its castle which stands high over the city; when floodlit at night it looks like a fairytale castle hovering above in the dark sky. Features of the castle include Saint Margaret's Chapel, the Great Hall, the Honours of Scotland and the Stone of Destiny as well as the national War Museum of Scotland and two regimental museums.

In the central and highest part of the Castle is the Scottish National War Memorial in which can be seen several monuments relating to New Zealand. This is probably the most magnificent war memorial in the world and was built with funds received from Scots at

The Scottish National War Memorial within the walls of Edinburgh Castle
Photograph: Trustees of the Scottish National War Memorial. There are several memorials here to New Zealand servicemen and on Anzac Day a remembrance service takes place at noon.

home and abroad. Every year on Anzac Day a ceremony of wreath laying takes place here at noon. Visitors from New Zealand are most welcome and are requested to be seated by 11.50 a.m. For further details, telephone (0131) 226-7393.

As one enters the War Memorial's Hall of Honour the lofty arch of the Shrine is straight ahead. Turning left one sees the memorial "To Scotsmen of all ranks who fell while serving with units of the British Dominions and Colonies, 1914-1918". As one looks at this memorial the stained glass window on the left represents Autumn while the one on the right is a representation of Winter.

On the other side of the Winter window is the West Bay which houses memorials to the Mercantile Marine, Women's Services, the Indian Army and others. One of the more interesting is a stone panel depicting canaries and mice – "The Tunnellers' Friends". While digging tunnels under no-man's land on the Western Front the tunnellers, including men of the New Zealand Tunnelling Company, took these small creatures with them for safety; in the event of the air becoming unfit to breathe they quickly became affected.

Crossing to the Shrine one sees the figure of Saint Michael the Archangel looking down on the steel Casket which contains the Roll of Honour of Scots killed while serving with British and Commonwealth forces. Around the Casket is a bronze frieze of servicemen and women of the 1914-1918 War; the seventh figure from the left on the Second panel is a piper of the 16th Waikato Company, Auckland Regiment.

The Castle Rock is exposed through the floor of the Shrine. On it stands the Stone of Remembrance on which is cut the Cross of Sacrifice and the words "Their Name Liveth".

On either side of the archway leading from the Shrine is carved a Tree of Empire; from its branches hang shields bearing the coats-of-arms of the dominions, including New Zealand's.

On the corner of Edinburgh's George Street and Castle Street is a statue of Doctor Thomas Chalmers after whom Port Chalmers in Dunedin is named. This powerful preacher and professor of theology became the first Moderator of the Free Church after the split of 1843 which in Presbyterian circles is known as "The Disruption". The rift between the Free Kirk and the Auld Kirk was not healed until 1929. Chalmers, championing the Free Church, opposed the imposition of a minister on a congregation without its approval. He died in the year that the Scottish pioneers sailed to Otago to establish a Free Church colony.

A further link with the founding of Otago can be seen at The Cross in the Grassmarket. To-day a peaceful cobbled street, it was formerly a place of execution. One of those whose last view of the world was this square that looks up to Edinburgh Castle was Donald Cargill, the Covenanter of fixed opinions, who denounced Charles II for "treachery, tyranny and lechery". He preached this subversive message until he was captured and executed on this spot for high treason on 27th July, 1681. His descendant was Captain William Cargill who, with Rev. Thomas Burns, the nephew of Scotland's poet, Robbie Burns, founded the settlement of Otago. Invercargill, as we have seen, was named after Captain Cargill. A flat, round stone marks the spot in the Grassmarket where Cargill and the other Covenanters were parted from this world.

However, Edinburgh's links with New Zealand go beyond Otago; for decades Edinburgh University was the preferred place of study for New Zealand doctors. Sir John Logan Campbell, the "Father of Auckland", attended its Medical School from 1834 to 1839. Logan Campbell lived at 17 Albany Street, in the New Town. For many decades from the founding of Otago College of the University of New Zealand (later Otago University), the only medical school in New Zealand, an aspiring doctor would study for two years at Otago and then go on to complete his studies at Edinburgh. One of the many who did so was Sir Truby King, the founder of the Plunket Society.

For those wishing to look up their Scottish ancestry the General Register Office for Scotland is in New Register House, West Register Street, Edinburgh, EH1 3TY (Tel: 0131-3340380).

A trip from the west end of Prince's Street along the main Glasgow road brings one to the prosperous suburb of Murrayfield with its fine Victorian buildings. Murrayfield is best known as the home of Scottish rugby and the ground where Colin Meads was sent off the field during the New Zealand-Scotland match on 2nd December, 1967. This dastardly deed was the work of

Irish referee, Kevin Kelleher, who shouldn't have even been at the match since he had smuggled himself into Britain in defiance of the emergency foot-and-mouth regulations that were in force at the time because of an outbreak of the disease in Ireland. It was in the closing minutes of the match when the referee sent off New Zealand's living legend for what he deemed "dangerous play" – one way, no doubt, for an otherwise forgettable referee to make a name for himself in rugby history.

Murrayfield was built after the First World War and was first used in the 1924-5 season. It has a heating system under the turf, which was the gift of a rich Scottish supporter in 1959. Who said the Scots are mean?

Murrayfield is situated in Roseburn Street, West Edinburgh. There are hour-long guided tours between 10 a.m. and 3 p.m. Tuesday-Thursday. There is also a souvenir shop

In recent years Scottish rugby has become increasingly dependent on New Zealand players; the Scots team of 2001 included five New Zealanders – the Leslie brothers, John and Martin, Gordon Simpson, Glen Metcalfe and Brendan Laney. Martin Leslie has had a long association with Edinburgh Rievers, a club that in 2001 signed on Todd Blackadder as well. In the pioneering period of the nineteenth century Scotland sent thousands of its people to New Zealand where they helped to build the country; the recent influx of New Zealand players into the Scottish rugby team is the "return gift".

EAST LOTHIAN

East Fortune

A short distance north-east of Haddington is the Scottish Museum of Flight at East Fortune. Not only is this well worth a visit for its wonderful collection of planes but in the entrance way to the main hall is a bronze plaque, mounted on kauri, in memory of those New Zealand airmen of the Second World War who died on operations from Scotland. At the bottom of the plaque are the words: "They Watch Over Scotia Still".

The plaque, unveiled in 2002, was an official Golden Jubilee project which was initiated by the Scottish branch of the New Zealand Society (U.K.). In the words of its President, Peter Leslie, "This commemoration is appropriately timed to coincide with our Sovereign's Golden Jubilee year with the defined link of 'service before self'."

The Museum of Flight is situated on a former R.A.F. operational base where several New Zealand air crew served during the War.

For some good Scottish fare try the museum's Parachute Café. It is run by Clarissa Dickson-Wright, one half of the *Two Fat Ladies* whose cooking programmes have appeared on New Zealand television. And, as Clarissa always says, "Don't forget to put plenty of cream on the scones!"

FIFE

Saint Andrew's

"Would you like to see a city given over,
Soul and body to a tyrannizing game?
If you would, there's little need to be a rover,
For Saint Andrew's is the abject city's name."

- R.F.Murray, *The City of Golf*

The town of Saint Andrew's on the coast of Fife is the traditional home of golf. Its famous Royal and Ancient Golf Club, founded in 1754, is the governing body that is responsible for the rules of golf.

Among the courses at Saint Andrew's are the Old, the New (1894), the Eden (1912) and the Jubilee. Golf has been played on the Old Course continuously for more than five centuries. It used to consist of twenty-two holes (eleven out and eleven back) but in 1764 was changed to eighteen holes and that is why every golf course has eighteen holes. To play on the course at Saint Andrew's it is not necessary to be a member or even to have an introduction but one must book well in advance. This can be done by writing to the Links Trust, Saint Andrew's, Fife KY16 9SF (or www.golfagent.com). You must give your name, club, handicap and the date(s) on which you wish to play.

The other thing that Saint Andrew's is famous for is its ancient university which, founded in 1411, is the oldest in Scotland and the third oldest in Britain after Oxford and Cambridge. This is where our future king, Prince William, commenced his studies in art history in October, 2001.

It was here that Bernard Freyberg, then a mere colonel, was given an honorary degree in Literature on 3rd May, 1922, in recognition of his outstanding bravery in the First World War. In his Address the Rector (Vice-Chancellor) spoke of the New Zealander's courage thus: "Courage is the thing. All goes if courage goes....Be not merely courageous, but light-hearted and gay."

GRAMPIANS

Huntly

On the A96 between Aberdeen and Inverness is the market town of Huntly from which the name of the Waikato town is derived. It was so named by a Scottish settler who hailed from Huntly in Scotland.

ANGUS

Glamis Castle

Situated a few miles north of Dundee on the A928 is the fairytale castle of Glamis, the ancestral home of the Queen Mother's family, the Earls of Strathmore. It is a place of ghostly legends and secrets. During the Jacobite rebellion of 1715 the Old Pretender, father of Bonnie Prince Charlie, held his court here – an interesting contrast to its later role as the childhood home of the Queen Mother, the most beloved queen of the Hanoverian line against whom the Old Pretender was rebelling! Princess Margaret was born within the castle walls in 1930. Glamis was originally a royal hunting lodge and was granted by King Robert II of Scotland to the Queen Mother's ancestor, Sir John Lyon in 1372.

The Wellington suburb of Strathmore, which was laid out in 1927 on the eve of her visit to New Zealand with her husband, the future King George VI, was named in her honour while its streets commemorate some of her family connections – Cavendish Square, Bentinck Avenue, Elphinstone Avenue, Tannadyce Street, Streatlam Crescent, Kinghorne Street and Glamis Avenue.

Arbroath

A few miles north-east of Dundee on the A92 is the seaside resort and fishing port of Arbroath (the second syllable is pronounced as in "growth"). It nestles beneath the ruins of its great abbey which was founded by King William the Lion in 1178. On the Sunday nearest Anzac Day there is a ceremony at 2 p.m. at the Western Cemetery at Arbroath where four New Zealand servicemen, who served in the Fleet Air Arm during the Second World War, are buried. They died while on operations from nearby Naval Air Stations.

ABERDEENSHIRE

Aberdeen

Traditionally known for its fish and granite, Aberdeen was the port of embarkation for some of the Scottish settlers who sailed to New Zealand. The city has many fine granite buildings that sparkle and look their best after a shower of rain. Marischal College, part of Aberdeen University, is widely regarded as the finest granite building in the world. People from Waipu in North Auckland might find this building material vaguely familiar; the Scottish Pioneers' Memorial in their town is made of Aberdeen granite.

In the 1970s and 1980s there were quite a few New Zealanders based in Aberdeen who worked on the offshore oil rigs in the North Sea. They formed a rugby team which played under the name "The Oil Blacks". This social team still plays one match a year.

ARGYLL

Oban

The main settlement of Oban on Stewart Island is named after the resort town of Oban on the west coast of Argyll from where the Caledonian MacBrayne ferries leave for the islands of Mull, Tiree, Coll, Barra and South Uist.

Inveraray

South-east of Oban and overlooking the waters of Loch Fyne is the fairytale castle of Inveraray, which is the home of the Duke of Argyll, the Chief of the Clan Campbell.

The visitor to Inveraray Castle can see the State Dining Room, the Tapestry Drawing Room, the Armoury Hall, Saloon, Clan Room and other features. The Clan Room contains family trees of the Clan Campbell as well as information for New Zealand Campbells on how to join the local Clan Campbell Society of New Zealand.

Inveraray Castle is open from the first Saturday in April to the second Sunday in October, Monday-Saturday from 10 a.m. to 5.45 p.m. and on Sundays 1-5.45 p.m. In April, May, June, September and October it is closed from 1-2 p.m. on Monday-Saturday.

Mull

With a population of only about 3,000 the island of Mull is very much a shadow of its former self; like the rest of the Highlands it underwent a process of massive depopulation during the "Clearances" of the late eighteenth and early nineteenth centuries. Ruined crofts and piles of stones can be seen on many parts of the island – the sad remains of once thriving settlements.

The island is the traditional home of the Clan MacLean whose head, Sir Lachlan MacLean, the twenty-eighth chief (since the thirteenth century), still lives at Duart Castle which stands as a landmark overlooking the Sound of Mull.

Many of the clansfolk who were uprooted sailed to New Zealand and settled in different parts – mainly in Otago and around Waipu in North Auckland. The result of this mass movement of people is that there are now more MacLeans, MacDonalds, MacKays and MacLeods in New Zealand than there are in the Highlands.

There are twice as many deer on Mull as people and it is also possible to see otters, seals and sea eagles as well as more than two hundred species of birds.

Mull can be reached by ferry from Oban. The voyage to Craignure on Mull takes 40 minutes.

Iona

"a nest of singing birds".

> - Saint Columba's description of Iona, c. 597 A.D.

Situated off the southern tip of the Isle of Mull, the smaller island of Iona is the holy place of Saint Columba who brought Christianity to Scotland from Ireland in 563 A.D. In the Reilig Odhrain (Saint Oran's Burial Ground) lie the remains of sixty kings – most of the early kings of Scotland as well as some Irish and

Norwegian monarchs. Between 795 and 806 A.D. Iona was ransacked three times by the Vikings who made a habit of seeking out defenceless monasteries and their gold; on the last occasion every member of the community was slaughtered at a place that is still known as Martyrs' Bay.

Iona is dominated by its ancient abbey which was described by Wordsworth as "this Glory of the West". Founded by the Benedictines at the beginning of the thirteenth century, it stands as a landmark overlooking the wild waters of the North Atlantic. However, after the Reformation it fell into disuse and neglect. The Abbey church was restored and the monks' old living quarters were rebuilt by the Iona Community, an ecumenical Christian group that was founded in 1938. The refectory of the Abbey has been restored as a result of financial contributions from New Zealand, while the timber used in refurbishing it was a gift from Norway.

The rise of Dun-I in the north of the island, although only 332 feet high, commands a magnificent view that includes Barra Head in the Outer Hebrides, the distant peaks of Rhum and Eigg, the Cuillin hills of Skye and the Paps of Jura in the south.

The journey to Iona from Oban involves two ferries and a bus across the island of Mull and there are several small hotels and cottages where visitors may enjoy the simple hospitality of the islanders. One of the nicest things about Iona is that cars are not encouraged and so the best way to explore this cradle of Scottish Christianity is on foot or by pony and trap. Thus one can savour the peace and beauty of the Hebridean seascape. Many visitors do not want to leave to return to "civilisation" but there is an old Gaelic saying that he who comes to Iona once will come three times.

Address: Iona Abbey, Isle of Iona, Argyll PA76 6SN. Tel: 01681-700404. Fax: 01681-700460. ionacomm@iona.org.uk

Skye

> "Speed, bonnie boat, like a bird on the wing,
> Onward, the sailors cry;
> Carry the lad that's born to be king
> Over the sea to Skye."
>
> - *The Skye Boat Song* alluding to Bonnie Prince Charlie's stay on Skye during the 1745 Jacobite rebellion.

It is now possible to drive across the new bridge to Skye instead of having to go "over the sea to Skye". Whether this new amenity, with its expensive toll, adds to the character of the island or not is a moot point.

Skye is the ancestral home of the McLeods of whom there are several thousand in New Zealand. The McLeods were frequently in conflict with other clans like the powerful McDonalds, who were Lords of the Isles, and a battle between these two families took place at Ardmore on Skye in May, 1578. Ardmore, the site of motor racing near Auckland, is named after this clan battle site. It can be reached from the Portree-Dunvegan road by turning on to the B886 near the Fairy Bridge and winding your way up the Vaternish peninsula to Trumpan which overlooks Ardmore Point.

The church at Trumpan is now a ruin. On the day of the battle the MacDonalds landed on the beach at Ardmore and torched this church where the McLeods were praying. Only one woman escaped; she raised the alarm whereupon McLeods came running from all directions, chased the murdering MacDonalds and killed every one of them. The enormity of the crime – killing people in a church – deprived the MacDonalds of Christian burials. From this remote site and bloody incident did Ardmore in Auckland get its name.

The MacLeods and MacDonalds still inhabit Skye although they live at opposite ends of the island, the MacLeod stronghold being Dunvegan Castle on the north-west coast while in the south-east, only a short walk from where the ferries arrive from Mallaig, are the ruins of Armadale Castle, the home of the MacDonalds of Sleat. At Armadale is the Clan Donald Centre that tells the story of this famous clan of which there are tens of thousands living in New Zealand.

In the Study Centre is a reference collection of over 6,000 books and documents which are a rich source of genealogical material for MacDonalds.

Included in the Clan Donald Centre is the Museum of the Isles which describes the turbulent history of the Highlands and islands, culminating in the Clearances which drove so many of the clansfolk to places like New Zealand. Armadale is sixteen miles south of Broadford on the scenic A851 route.

ROSS

Easter Fearn

It was in the small Highland village of Easter Fearn, thirty miles north of Inverness in Rosshire, that New Zealand's Prime Minister during the Second World War, Peter Fraser, was born on 28th August, 1884. His father was the local bootmaker who worked from a room in the family home, a cottage which is still standing. Known as Fraser Cottage, it is on the corner of Finlayson Street and Rhynie Road and there is a plaque recording Peter Fraser's association with it. Today it is a private residence. To be the Prime Minister of a country at war seemed a strange destiny for a man who was convicted of sedition and sentenced to a year's imprisonment for opposing conscription in the First World War.

Fraser was a socialist who worked his way up through the Labour movement to take over the prime ministership on the death of Michael Savage. As national leader during the Second World War Fraser and his government faced the possibility of invasion of New Zealand by Japan. It was only the merciful intervention of American naval power at Guadalcanal that stopped the Japanese advance and turned the tide of the Pacific War.

In Fearn the future Prime Minister of New Zealand attended the local school, which can be seen opposite his cottage. He then worked first as the village postman and later as an apprentice carpenter. Times were hard and Fraser found solace in socialism.

When he became Prime Minister in 1940 the people of Fearn sent him an illuminated address; he visited the village in 1941 to a hero's welcome.

Easter Fearn is reached by taking the A9 north of Inverness and then turning left on to the A836.

Croick

A few miles west of Fearn on the A836 one sees the secondary road leading to Croick. This tiny village was not always as silent and empty as it is to-day; before the Highland Clearances there were many more people.

The village church was built in 1827 by the great engineer, Thomas Telford. It had a congregation of more than two hundred who were drawn from nearby crofting communities. In 1845 all these people were evicted from their land and they had no choice but to emigrate to Canada, Australia and New Zealand. Before leaving, they gathered in their church for a final service and scratched their names and comments on the east windows – one of the few ways that they could make their feelings known.

SUTHERLAND

Clachtoll

On the coast at Clachtoll (on the A837 north of Ullapool) is a memorial in the form of a block of local marble to Rev. Norman McLeod (1780-1866), who was born here.

McLeod was one of the oddest characters ever to sail to New Zealand, This renegade minister of the Presbyterian Church emigrated first to Nova Scotia in Canada with a band of disciples. At Saint Ann's on Cape Breton Island, Nova Scotia, he built a church from which he used to enliven the otherwise boring lives of his backwoodsmen parishioners with three hour "fire and brimstone" sermons in which he denounced individual parishioners for misdeeds that they had allegedly committed during the week. On one occasion he even scolded his own wife from the pulpit because she had dared to wear a coloured ribbon in her hat on the Sabbath.

In the 1860s he and almost a thousand Scots from Nova Scotia sailed to New Zealand in six ships, some of which they built themselves. Many of them settled at Waipu in Northland where there is a museum in honour of them and their weird pastor.

The memorial here at Clachtoll looks out over the Atlantic which is particularly appropriate since that was the first of three oceans that McLeod and his fellow Scots had to cross on their long and interrupted journey from Scotland to New Zealand.

SHETLAND ISLANDS

These far north islands, famed for birds, fish and Shetland ponies, were Danish until 1469 and some Viking traditions still thrive. The reason for the change of sovereignty was that the Shetlands, together with the Orkneys, were pledged to James III of Scotland for the dowry of his wife, Margaret of Denmark.

The islands are a paradise for bird-watchers; the birds fly thousands of miles to summer in the Shetlands – even terns from the Antarctic. There are also bright beaked puffins, gannets, razorbills, shags, great skuas and many others.

In the nineteenth century quite a few Shetlanders emigrated to New Zealand even though they had further to travel than other emigrants. Among those who sailed to New Zealand was Robert Stout, who later became Prime Minister and Chief Justice. He was also a Prohibitionist, seeking to rid mankind of the Demon Drink. Since the name he bore was that of a particularly fine beverage brewed by Guinness, Stout was a somewhat incongruous prohibitionist.

He was born in Lerwick, the main town of the Shetlands, and attended both the parish school and Lerwick Academy where, like so many other founders of New Zealand, he shone in the Classics. The cobbled streets and old stone buildings of Lerwick are still very much as they were in Stout's day. Wellington's Stout Street, headquarters of New Zealand's rapidly disappearing defence forces, is named after him as is the Stout Research Centre at Victoria University, of which he was a founder.

To-day the population of the Shetlands is 23,000; there are, however, more than 80,000 people in New Zealand who are of Shetland descent.

WALES

Because of a shared love of rugby Wales and New Zealand have always had a very special relationship. Plus, of course, the proliferation of Welsh names like Jones, Morgan, Thomas, Edwards and Davies throughout New Zealand are testimony of the enormous Welsh contribution to the New Zealand bloodstock. Definitely a place where a New Zealander will feel very much at home.

GLAMORGAN

Cardiff

The main stop for most New Zealanders in South Wales is Cardiff or, more specifically, Cardiff Arms Park (now referred to by the less romantic title "the Millennium Stadium") which has been the scene of so many memorable moments in Test matches between the All Blacks and the Welsh and the All Blacks and the Barbarians.

Situated on the banks of the River Taff, this home of Welsh rugby is right in the heart of the city – even closer to the pubs and shops than Wellington's new stadium. And not nearly so windy! What distinguishes a Test match at Cardiff is the atmosphere – the singing, the cheering and the powerful emotion.

It was here that one of the most controversial and talked about incidents in New Zealand rugby history occurred – the try by Bob Deans in 1905 that was disallowed by the referee. Down 3-0 and with only a few minutes left, New Zealand's Billy Wallace caught a Welsh kick near the half-way line and set off on an amazing run through most of the Welsh team. About twenty yards from the goal posts he could go no further so he passed the ball to Deans who scored right under the posts.

Unfortunately, by the time the referee arrived on the scene Deans had been pulled back and appeared to be six inches short of the line. The referee, Mr. Dallas of Scotland, who was wearing a Norfolk shooting jacket, knickerbockers and tweed cap, disallowed the try and New Zealand lost the match. However, if he had allowed the try, we would not still be talking about it and a legend, which gives both Welsh and New Zealanders a common point of reference, would not have been born.

The after-match atmosphere in the nearby pubs has always been lively; the Welsh are probably the most friendly, warm and convivial race in the world. And they love their rugby just as much as New Zealanders. Problem is that they just can't stop talking! If you get as far as the Angel Hotel in Castle Street, don't forget to drink a toast to All Black, Keith Murdoch, who punched a security guard in the hotel kitchen during the

1972-3 tour of Britain. For this epic deed Murdoch was sent home by the All Blacks management but in view of the obnoxious attitude of goons in pubs he should really have been given a medal.

Bordering Cardiff's great rugby ground and running along the nearby river path is the Millennium Walk which was established at the time of the Rugby World Cup in 1999. Specific areas of paving are dedicated to the various countries whose teams played in the World Cup and the names of all the team members are included. In each area a mosaic was designed to represent the character of the particular country and the one for New Zealand was the work of the pupils and teachers of Ysgol Mynydd Bychan, a Welsh language school that is situated in New Zealand Road in the Cardiff inner city suburb of Maindy.

For those of Welsh blood who want to investigate their lineage the records for this part of South Wales are held at the Glamorgan Record Office, Glamorgan Building, King Edward VII Avenue, Cathay's Park (not far from Cardiff Castle). Tel: (029) 2078-0282. There are two search rooms open to the public.

CARMARTHEN

Carmarthen

Continuing west from Cardiff one reaches the large town of Carmarthen which was a regional centre in Roman times. Part of the ramparts and amphithreatre built by the Romans can still be seen.

Of particular interest to New Zealanders is the Picton Memorial, which stands on a traffic island at the top of Picton Terrace, not far from Carmarthen Park. The memorial is to General Sir Thomas Picton, a native of Carmarthen, who was a hero of the Peninsular War but was later killed while leading his division to victory at Waterloo in 1815. Picton, at the top of the South Island, was named in his honour.

General Picton's medals from both the Peninsula War and Waterloo are on display at the County Museum at Abergwili, two miles east of the town centre. The museum also has exhibits on Carmarthen's Roman history.

Picton's portrait is on display at the Guildhall, Carmarthen, while the shell of Iscoed, his house at Ferryside, can be seen from the Llanstephan Road, south of the town.
(See: Saint Paul's, London).

PEMBROKE

Milford Haven

West of Carmarthen on the A40 is the town of Haverfordwest from which one can drive south to the port of Milford Haven which is really a drowned valley ("The Haven") that forms the harbour entrance. When whalers first entered the Sounds of Fiordland at the bottom of the South Island in the 1820s some of them noted the resemblance to the drowned valley at Milford Haven, which is not surprising since the Sound, which they named "Milford" after Milford Haven, was similarly created when the sea flooded a valley that had become unusually deep as a result of glacial action. That is how Milford Sound got its name.

NORTHERN IRELAND

Just as twelve Presidents of the United States can claim descent from the small Protestant population of Northern Ireland so too has this relatively tiny community provided New Zealand with some of its most distinguished Prime Ministers.

BELFAST

Although many Northern Irish have settled in New Zealand there was only one organised emigration from the province and that was the settlement of the Katikati district near Tauranga in 1875. This was the brainchild of George Vesey Stewart and most of the 238 settlers who left Belfast Docks on board the *Carisbrooke Castle* on 8th June, 1875, were tenant farmers and their families. Three years later another sailing ship, the *Lady Jocelyn*, brought another batch of Ulster folk to Katikati.

Those of Ulster descent can trace their roots at the General Register Office, 49 Chichester Street, Belfast, where birth and death records as far back as

1864 are kept as well as marriage certificates from 1922 onwards.

The town of Belfast, just out of Christchurch, is named after this capital of Northern Ireland.

ANTRIM

Glenavy

Two miles from Glenavy on the A30 and seven miles north-west of Lisburn is the farmhouse where John Ballance, the son of a tenant farmer, was born in 1839. Ballance was the Liberal leader who was Prime Minister of New Zealand from 1890 until his death in 1893. He was educated at Wilson's Academy in Belfast. Wellingtonians will be familiar with Ballance as one of the two statues in the grounds of Parliament is of this reforming Prime Minister.

The farmhouse where Ballance was born is situated at 118a Lisburn Road, Glenavy. It also serves as the Honorary Consulate for New Zealand in Northern Ireland.

The building has been restored with the parlour being furnished in the style of the time when Ballance lived there. There is also a Tea Barn for refreshments and a gift shop. These are housed in one of the nineteenth century barns on the property. Behind the house is the Old Orchard which has recently been replanted with fruit trees of nineteenth century varieties. The present trees were planted by members of the All Black team when they were touring Ireland in 1989.

Whether they used shovels or their boots I have not been able to ascertain. There are guided tours of Ballance House which is open from April to September, Tuesday-Friday 11-5, Week-ends and Bank Holidays, 2 – 5 p.m. (Tel: 01846-648492)

LONDONDERRY

Limavady

Another Ulster born Prime Minister was William Ferguson Massey (1856-1925) who was the Reform Party Prime Minister during the difficult days of the First World War and who represented New Zealand at the Versailles Peace Conference in 1919 (See: National Portrait Gallery, London). Massey was born to poor parents on 26th August, 1856, in Irish Green Street, Limavady. The house is no longer standing and its exact site is unknown. However, there is a commemorative plaque on a wall beside the Spar shop on Irish Green Street.

In 1870 William Massey emigrated to New Zealand where he succeeded through hard work. The story is often told of how he was working on top of a haystack on his farm just out of Auckland when the telegram arrived informing him that he was to be Prime Minister. It was spiked on to the end of a pitchfork and handed up to him. He thus became Prime Minister while on top of a haystack! Massey in west Auckland and Massey University in Palmerston North are named after him and he is buried in splendid surroundings at

Statue of William Massey at Limavady
Prime Minister of New Zealand in the First World War, Massey was born in the Northern Ireland town of Limavady.

Massey Memorial above Wellington Harbour – a whole world away from his humble birth place here in Limavady.

Massey returned to Limavady twice and there is a full size bronze statue of him outide the Council Offices in Connell Street, Limavady. Since Connell Street runs into Irish Green Street the statue is just around the corner from where he was born.

Situated on the Roe River, Limavady is a picturesque town of Georgian houses and shops. It can be reached on the A2 north of Londonderry.

CHANNEL ISLANDS

Jersey

Well-known as the setting for the *Bergerac* series which was shown on New Zealand television some years ago, Jersey is a delightful and prosperous island in the English Channel.

The main town is Saint Helier after which the Auckland bayside suburb is named. The island has long been a centre for banking and other financial services but is now under attack by the E.U. monolith which has such an aversion for small units like Gibraltar, Monaco and the Channel Islands.

Jersey is one of the oldest possessions of the Crown and was formerly part of the Duchy of Normandy whence William the Conqueror came in 1066. When the Channel Islanders drink the Loyal Toast, it is to "The Queen, Our Duke".

The character of Jersey is a mixture of English and French. Over the centuries these islands have produced generations of fishermen who used to sail across the Atlantic to fish the Newfoundland Banks. Some of these seamen ventured further afield and finished up in faraway places like New Zealand; they can usually be identified by their French surnames.

AUTOGRAPHS

One of the joys of travelling and meeting new people is exchanging autographs. I have deliberately left these pages for signatures and, to start your collection, have included the autographs of some of people who figure prominently in the guide.

Jamˢ Cook

Captain Cook

R Seddon

Richard John Seddon

Anthony F Wilding

Anthony Wilding

Katherine Mansfield

Katherine Mansfield

B C Freyberg

General Freyberg

AUTOGRAPHS

INDEX OF NEW ZEALAND TOWNS

Alfriston, Auckland, 107-8
Ashburton, 139-140
Auckland, 21, 43, 69, 97, 100, 105, 108, 146, 157, 197, 217, 238-9, 256, 274, 286
Balclutha, 257
Banks Peninsula, 20, 25, 141, 175
Belfast, 285
Birkenhead, Auckland, 217
Blenheim, 184-5
Canterbury, 28, 33, 38, 45-8, 99, 101-2, 144, 153, 162-5, 167-8, 174-5, 195
Christchurch, 46, 59, 101, 105, 108, 132, 135, 159, 162-4, 167, 175, 196-7, 200, 252
Clive, 21, 64-5, 156
Cobden, Greymouth, 22
Collingwood, 44, 241-2
Cromwell, 69
Devonport, Auckland, 146
Dunedin, 23, 102-3, 108, 251, 259-60, 262
Epsom, Auckland, 108
Foxton, 38, 240-1
Gisborne, 97, 192, 209, 227
Gladstone, 37
Greymouth, 22, 43
Greytown, 43
Hamilton, 30
Hastings, 22, 66, 73, 107, 158
Havelock, 20
Houhora, 35
Howick, Auckland, 100, 184, 245
Huntly, 268
Invercargill, 194, 263
Kaipara, 100
Katikati, 284
Kelburn, Wellington, 253

Kilbirnie, Wellington, 255
Kimbolton, 173
Lichfield, 204
Marlborough Sounds, 143, 197
Marton, 229
Milford Sound, 283-4
Mosgiel, 251
Mount Eden, Auckland, 239
Napier, 19, 44, 65, 130, 156
Naseby, 174
Nelson, 18, 24, 34, 43-4, 68, 97, 99, 129, 240
New Brighton, Christchurch, 108
New Plymouth, 38, 59, 142-3
Oban, Stewart Island, 270
Onehunga, Auckland, 100
Onslow, Wellington, 116
Otago, 99, 152, 174, 257, 259-64
Otahuhu, Auckland, 100
Otira, 87, 153
Otorohonga, 148
Palmerston, 70-1, 286
Picton, 44, 283
Port Chalmers, 262
Queen Charlotte Sound, 141-2
Riccarton, Christchurch, 252
Richmond, 89
Roseneath, Wellington, 258
Rotorua, 116, 149
Royal Oak, Auckland, 199
Russell, 22
St. Albans, Christchurch, 159
St. Heliers, Auckland, 287
Stratford, 193-4
Strathmore, Wellington, 268
Sumner, Christchurch, 101
Taitapu, Christchurch, 46
Tauranga, 130, 203, 236, 284

Thames, 36, 47, 98, 182-4
Timaru, 32, 122
Torbay, Auckland, 140
Trentham, 207
Waiouru, 205
Waipu, 270, 278
Waitangi, 39, 114, 156
Waiuku, 41
Wakatipu, Lake, 88
Wanganui, 34, 68, 81, 110-1, 113, 127, 151, 187
Warkworth, 242-4
Wellington, 22, 41, 43-4, 77-8, 97, 99, 102, 105, 113, 115, 17, 143, 151, 155, 188-9, 203, 219, 227-8, 234, 239, 246, 253, 255-6, 258, 268, 279, 285
Weymouth, Auckland, 136
Whangarei, 197
Whitianga, 234-5

GENERAL INDEX

Aberdeen, 270
Abingdon, 182-4
Alfriston, Sussex, 107-8
Apsley House, London, 77-80
Arbroath, 269
Ardmore, 273-4
Ashburton, 139-40
Auckland, Earl of, 238-9
Ballance, John, 219, 285-6
Banks, Sir Joseph, 21, 25-6, 83, 85-7, 97, 119, 177, 214-5
Barking, 53-4
Bath, 155-6
Bealey, Samuel, 164-5
Belfast, 284-5
Bell, Sir Francis Dillon, 163
Bere Ferrers, 147

Birmingham, 186, 197
Bishop Auckland, 238-9
Blake, Sir Peter, 128, 131
Bledisloe, Lord, 39, 119, 156-7, 178
Blenheim Palace, 184-5
Blundell, Sir Denis, 40
Bodmin, 150-1
Boscobel House, 199-200
Bowen, Sir George, 181
Boyce, Raymond, 57
Brighton, 108
Brockenhurst, Hamps, 132-4
Brookwood Military Cemetery, 112
Brownlie, Cyril, 89
Bulford, Wilts, 137-9
Burghley House, 211-2
Burns, Rev. Thomas, 251, 263
Burwash, Sussex, 105-7
Butler, Samuel, 163
Cairns, Chris, 210
Cambridge, 160-72
Campbell, Sir John Logan, 69, 264
Cannock Chase, 204-6
Canterbury, 101-2
Cardiff, 280-2
Cargill, Donald, 257, 262
Cargill, Captain William, 99, 258, 264
Carmarthen, 282-3
Carsethorne, 250
Cavalry Memorial, Hyde Park, 80
Cenotaph, London, 64
Chaffers, Captain Edward, 144
Chalmers, Doctor Thomas, 263
Charing Cross Road, London, 24, 25
Charles, Bob, 222
Chester, 216
Christchurch, Dorset, 135

Chichester, Sir Francis, 74, 97-8
Churchill, Sir Winston, 42, 67, 69-70, 129, 184-5
Clachtoll, 278
Clandon Park, 114-117
Clive, Robert, 22, 64-5, 156
Clyde, 254-5
Coates, Gordon, 73, 163
Cobden, Richard, 22
Cobham, Lord, 119, 165, 195-7
Codford Saint Mary's, Wilts, 136
Collingwood, Admiral, 44, 241-2
Cook, Captain, 21, 52-5, 74, 76, 96-98, 128-9, 141-2, 168-172, 228-235
Cooke, Lord, 38, 68, 165
Covent Garden, London, 29-30
Coventry, 186-190
Croick, 277
Crowthorne, Berks, 117
Dartmouth, 140
Daylesford, Gloucs., 158-9
Deans brothers, John and William, 252
Deans, Bob, 252, 281
Deans, Bruce and Robbie, 252
Derby, 207-210
Devonport, 146
Domett, Alfred, 38, 65
Durham, 235-8
Durham, Earl of, 98, 239-240, 246
East Fortune, 266
East Grinstead, 103-4
Easter Fearn, 276-7
Edinburgh, 259-265
Elworthy, Lord, 32-3, 35, 68, 121-2, 165
Emsworth, Hamps., 128
Epsom, 108-9
Eton, 118-9
Falmouth, 152-4

Farsley, Leeds, 224-5
Fawkes, Guy, 66, 94-95, 99, 226
Fearn (See: Easter Fearn)
Fergusson. Sir Bernard, 119, 193
Fergusson, Sir Charles, 252
Fergusson, Sir James, 193
Fitzgerald, James Edward, 167-8
Fitzroy, Governor Robert, 37
Fownhope, 201
Fox, Sir William, 38, 240-1
Fraser, Peter, 46-48, 68, 80, 129, 276-7
Freyberg, Lord, 18, 44, 68, 70, 71-2, 88, 97, 114, 122, 180, 194, 214, 267
Gisborne, William, 193, 209
Glamis Castle, 268-9
Glasgow, 256-8
Glasgow, Earl of, 253
Glenavy, 285-6
Globe Theatre, 56-60
Gloucester, 157
Godley, John Robert, 28, 135, 175, 195
Gravesend, 98-101
Gray's Inn, London, 40-41
Great Ayton, 230-1
Greenock, 256
Greenwich, 96-8
Gretna Green, 248-251
Grey, Lord, 245-6
Grey, Lord of Nuneaton, 68
Grey, Sir George, 43, 245
Guildford, 112-4
Guildhall, London, 46
Hadlee, Sir Richard, 210
Hagley Hall, Worcs., 196-7
Hampstead Heath, 92-5
Harper, Henry John Chitty, 118
Harrogate, 226-8

Hastings, Sussex, 107
Hastings, Warren, 22, 66, 73, 107, 158-9
Havelock, Sir Henry, 19
Hendon, R.A.F. Museum, 95
Hereford, 200-1
Hillary, Sir Edmund, 120-1
Hobson, Captain, 199, 237
Holland, Sir Sidney, 72
Holyoake, Sir Keith, 121
Hooker, Sir Joseph, 86-7
Howick, 245-6
Hulme, Keri, 47-48
Huntly, 268
Hutton, John, 113, 125, 187-8
Hyde Park, 80-81
Imperial War Museum, 59
Inner Temple, London, 37-38
Inverary Castle, 271
Iona, 272-4
Jellicoe, Earl of, 21, 23, 44
Jersey, 288
Julius, Bishop Churchill, 180
Kelburn Castle, 252-5
Kensington, 81-3
Kew Gardens, 85-8
Kidderminster, 198
Kilbirnie, 255
Kimbolton, 173
King, Sir Truby, 263
Kipling, Rudyard, 105-8
Kirk, David, 179, 181
Laidlaw, Chris, 177, 179
Leeds, 224-5
Leslie, Peter, 266
Lewis, Chris, 85
Lewis, John, 119
Lichfield, 201-4

Limavady, 286-7
Lincoln, 212-4
Little Bowden, 174-5
Little Coxwell, 184
Liverpool, 216-9
Looe, Cornwall, 149-150
Lords Cricket Ground, 92-3
Lovelock, Jack, 179-80
Low, Sir David, 83
Lush, Rev. Vicesimus, 184
Lydney Park, 156-7
Lytham Saint Anne's, 222
MacDonald, George Ranald, 177
McIndoe, Sir Archibald, 23, 35, 103-4
McIntyre, Peter, 93, 260
McKinnon, Ian, 119
McLeod, Rev. Norman, 278
Major, Dame Malvina, 30
Manchester, 222
Mansfield, Katherine, 27-8, 93-4, 149-150, 179
Marsden, Rev. Samuel, 161-2, 224-5
Marton, 228-230
Massey, William, 22, 90, 163, 286-7
Meads, Colin, 264
Middlesborough, 226-8
Milford Haven, 283-4
Molesworth, Sir William, 150-1
Montgomery, Field-Marshal, 23, 61
Moorhouse, William Sefton, 38
Mossgiel, 251
Mount Edgcumbe House, 147-9
Mulgan, Alan, 39, 44, 64, 160, 177
Mulgan, John, 177
Mull, 271-2
Murdoch, Keith, 281
Murrayfield, 263-4
Napier, Sir Charles, 19, 44, 65, 130, 156

National Portrait Gallery, London, 20
Naseby, 174
Nash, Walter, 198
Nelson, Admiral Horatio, 18, 44, 129
New Zealand House, 17
Newall, Lord, 23, 32
Newcastle-upon-Tyne, 241
Nottingham, 210
Nunneley, Kathleen, 174-5
Oban, 270
Old Bailey, London, 41
Onslow, Lord, 26, 114-7
Oxford, 174-80
Palmerston, Lord, 70-71, 82
Park, Sir Keith, 36-7, 46
Parun, Onny, 85
Pencarrow, 150-1
Picton, Sir Thomas, 44, 283
Plymouth, 141-6
Porritt, Lord, 68, 178
Portland, Isle of, 135-6
Portsmouth, 128-131
Privy Council, 62-63
Queen's College, Harley Street, London, 27
Rhodes, Cecil, 178
Rhodes, Sir Heaton, 46, 179
Rhodes-Moorhouse, William, 33-5
Riccarton, 252
Richmond, 85, 88
Richmond Park, 88-89
Richmond, C.W., 38
Rolleston, William, 167
Rosneath, 258
Rugby, 178, 190-4
Runnymede, 123-6
Rutherford, Lord, 24, 68, 72, 166, 222
St.Albans, Herts, 159

St. Andrew-the-Great, Cambridge, 168-171
St. Andrews (Royal and Ancient), 267-8
St. Bride's, London, 41
St. Clement Danes, London, 30-37
St. George's, Hanover Square, London, 26
St. Helens, Lancs, 219-222
St. Helier, 286
St. Lawrence Jewry, London, 48-50
St. Margaret's, Barking, 54-6
St. Paul's Cathedral, 42-6
Sanders, Dawn, 57
Sanders, William, V.C., 145
Sanders Cup, 20, 146
Savoy Hotel, London, 29
Seddon, R.J., 43, 75, 219-222
Selwyn, Bishop, 26, 162, 201-3
Shetland Islands, 279-80
Shipton-under-Wychwood, Oxfordshire, 185
Skye, 274-5
Sling Camp, 137-9
Soho Square, London, 25-26
South Shields, 240-139-40
Southampton, 132
Speakers' Corner, Hyde Park, 80-81
Stafford, 206
Staithes, 231-2
Stones, Anthony, 97, 157
Stout, Sir Robert, 279-80
Stratford-upon-Avon, 194-5
Sullivan, Ven. Martin, 42
Sumner, Archbishop, 45, 101
Sunderland, 239-40
Sutherland, Dame Joan, 30
Te Kanawa, Dame Kiri, 29-30, 45, 83, 181
Thomas, Brian, 42, 73
Tidworth, 139
Todd, Mark, 211

Torpoint, 147-9
Torquay, 140
Trent, Squadron Leader, 34
Trentham, 207
Trigg, Lloyd, 35
Twickenham, 89-92
Tynemouth, 242
Virginia Water, 110-1
Wakefield, Captain Arthur, 99
Wakefield, Edward Gibbon, 40-41, 150, 163, 239, 248-50
Wakefield, Colonel William, 144, 150, 238
Walton-upon-Thames, 109-110
Ward, Sergeant James, 34
Warkworth, 242-5
Warrington, Lancs, 219
Webb Ellis, William, 179-80, 190-2
Wellington, Somerset, 155
Wellington, Duke of, 22, 43-4, 77-79, 119, 155
Wellington College, 18, 67, 117
Wellington Shakespeare Society, 56,
Westminster Abbey, 71
Weymouth, 136
Whitby, 232-5
Wilding, Anthony, 38, 84-5, 164, 200
Wilson, Sir John Cracroft, 179
Wimbledon, 84-5
Winchester, 131-2
Windsor, 118-122
Woking, 112
York, 225-6